THE DARK SIDE OF THE SUPERNATURAL

Other books by Bill Myers

Teen Series

Forbidden Doors

Dark Powers
Ancient Forces
Deadly Loyalty
Invisible Terror

Teen Nonfiction

Get Real
Hot Topics, Tough Questions

Adult Novels

Blood of Heaven
Threshold
Fire of Heaven
Eli
The Face of God
The Wager
When the Last Leaf Falls
Soul Tracker
The Presence
The Seeing
The Voice
Angel of Wrath
The God Hater
The Judas Gospel
Supernatural Love
Supernatural War

Kids' Series

McGee and Me
My Life As ...
Secret Agent Dingledorf
Bloodhounds, Inc.
The Elijah Project
Imager Chronicles
Bug Parables
T.J. and the Time Stumblers

THE DARK SIDE OF THE SUPERNATURAL

written by BILL MYERS & DAVE WIMBISH

ZONDERVAN

The Dark Side of the Supernatural

This title is also available as a Zondervan ebook. Visit www.zondervan.com/ebooks.

Requests for information should be addressed to:
Zondervan, *Grand Rapids, Michigan 49530*

ISBN: 978-0-310-73002-6

Published in association with the literary agency of Alive Communications, Inc., 7680 Goddard Street, Suite 200, Colorado Springs, CO 80920. www.alivecommunications.com

Cover design: Jeff Gifford

Printed in the United States of America

12 13 14 15 16 17 /DCI/ 20 19 18 17 16 15 14 13 12 11 10 9 8 7 6 5 4 3 2 1

For Diane:
an inspiration for us both.

Table of Contents

1

Supernatural Hunger

We all have it—this hunger, this yearning for something more. After all we're human, and humans are made of three parts …

Physical, mental … *and spiritual.*

And between eating and school and eating and work and eating and sports and eating and parents and friends—and did I mention eating?—we've pretty well got the first two parts of who we are covered.

But what about the third? The spiritual?

As a screenwriter, it seems every time I turn around, someone is asking me to come up with a story about the supernatural. And it's not just movies. Just check out TV, the Internet, local bookstores, or even music.

Everybody's hungry for answers. Especially …

Teenagers

Every day I get emails from students with questions: Are there ghosts? Are séances wrong? What about the glowing figure in my room? Are Ouija boards bad? What about UFOs? And on and on ...

Some of these questions come from teens who read my Forbidden Doors book series. In these twelve books, a teenage brother and sister become reluctant ghost busters and learn many of the truths about the supernatural that we'll be discussing here. Other emails come from students who have been frightened by actual encounters. Still others come from teenagers who have friends caught up in the stuff and want to help.

Instead of spending many hours a week answering the same questions over and over, I figured, why not put the info into one, easy-to-use reference book—something you can pull down from the shelf and get a quick overview and answers to the questions that come up in your life?

So in the coming chapters we'll explore the major supernatural beliefs and practices of today ... finding out which ones are real, which ones are bogus, and how to deal with them.

Real or Fake

As an author and filmmaker, I've spent years researching the paranormal—interviewing witches, Wiccans, psychics, and the head of the CIA's psychic research department. I have observed and participated in an exorcism, and hung out with a serial killer, those involved in ghost hunting, and UFO abductees. I have visited a top psychic lab, filmed miracles in third-world countries, and, of course, read thousands of accounts of supernatural events.

For the most part the stories of the supernatural are like mist. They vanish into nothing when you try to verify them.

But occasionally, there are situations that defy rational explanation and hold up under investigation.

There *are* haunted locations where chains rattle and disembodied voices can be heard whispering in the night.

There *are* people who receive messages from "beyond" through trances, automatic writing, and other means.

There *are* unexplainable things seen in the sky at night.

Good or Evil

Evidence proves there is a supernatural world out there. In fact, the Bible says as much. It also says that there's a good side to the supernatural and an evil side—a side that wants to help us and legitimately fill our hunger ... and a side that wants to destroy us.

Jesus Christ put it best when he said, "The thief comes only to steal and kill and destroy; I have come that they may have life, and have it to the full" (John 10:10).

Pretty intense words. Jesus was either lying or telling the truth. And if he's telling the truth, then there really is a thief out there—an enemy who wants to steal from us, who wants to kill us, and who wants to destroy us.

The good news is we don't have to be afraid of the thief, because we really do have Somebody who's on our side, Somebody who wants to protect us ... Somebody who will give us life.

The bad news is someone is also out to deceive us. So we can't go running after everything that's supernatural without considering the consequences. As I tell the high school and college students I work with, "Just because it glows in the dark doesn't make it good."

In fact, it's often just the opposite.

Our enemy Satan is alive and well, and he'll use everything in his power to draw people away from God ... including supernatural "special effects." Jesus again put it best when he said, "For false messiahs and false prophets will appear and perform great signs and wonders to deceive, if possible, even the elect" (Matthew 24:24).

And while I'm in a Bible-quoting mood, check this out: "The coming of the lawless one will be in accordance with how Satan works. He will use all sorts of displays of power through signs and wonders that serve the lie, and in all the ways wickedness deceives those who are perishing. They perish because they refused to love the truth and so be saved" (2 Thessalonians 2:9–10).

Same Old, Same Old

Lots of times young people are attracted to the supernatural because they have hard lives, or they don't fit in, or people treat them badly. As a result, it's only natural for them to be hungry for more power, to feel like they're special, to have their eyes opened with more insight. And their enemy, the thief who wants to kill and destroy, is only too happy to swoop in with his own brand of poisoned food, promising to make them more God-like.

It's the same old promise he's offered since the beginning of time: "When you eat of it your eyes will be opened, and you will be like God ..." (Genesis 3:5).

A Tricky Balance

C. S. Lewis, author of The Chronicles of Narnia, put the supernatural in perspective when he wrote, "There are two equal and opposite errors into which our race can fall about devils. One is to disbelieve in their existence. The other is to believe, and to feel an excessive and unhealthy interest in them."[1]

Lewis spoke of "devils," but we can easily replace the word with "the occult" or "the dark side of the supernatural." Yes, it's important to know what's going on, to be aware of Satan's tricks in today's world.

Aware of it … yes.

Fascinated by it … no.

The purpose of this book is not to draw attention to Satan or bring him glory. It's to expose him as the deceiving fraud he is and to unveil his schemes so *none* of us are fooled.

One Final Point

Finally, before we start, remember this:

Even though there's danger in the world of the supernatural, there's no power anywhere that comes close to the power of God or his Word. If you're a child of God, there's nothing Satan and all the powers of darkness can do to hurt you.

Nothing.

Again, quoting Jesus: "No one will snatch them out of my hand. My Father, who has given them to me, is greater than all; no one can snatch them out of my Father's hand" (John 10:28–29).

Jesus promised that if we belong to him, we actually have the power to beat the bad guys. In fact, if you were to meet Satan in a dark alley and you had a right relationship with God, the *devil* would be the one scared spitless. Mark 16:17 says, "And these signs will accompany those who believe: In my name they will drive out demons."

Or as one of Jesus' disciples put it, "The one who is in you is greater than the one who is in the world" (1 John 4:4).

That's what I hope to do with this book: expose today's supernatural counterfeits and equip you to beat them.

---

1. C. S. Lewis, The Screwtape Letters (New York: The MacMillan Company, 1959), 3.

2

Angels—The Good and the Bad

Angels are a big deal. In fact, the Bible mentions them approximately three hundred times.

The word actually means *messenger.* And, from the looks of things, that's their main function:

- The angel of the Lord talked to Moses in the burning bush.
- An angel told Mary she was going to give birth to the Messiah.
- Angels sang in the skies over Bethlehem to announce Christ's birth.
- An angel will sound the last trumpet, proclaiming the day of God's judgment.

So, aren't *all* angels good? Not according to the Bible.

Angel of Light

Scripture seems to indicate that Satan himself was once a top angel and that he's still capable of disguising himself as an angel of light (2 Corinthians 11:14). And, though the Bible doesn't get into specifics, it tells us that somewhere back in time Satan was filled with pride and led a revolt against God.

It seems pride is a huge deal with Satan. He had status; he had standing. But it wasn't enough. Somehow, he used his clout to get one-third of all the angels to join with him in an insane attempt to overthrow God. Talk about an ego.

The Book of Revelation puts it this way:

> Then war broke out in heaven. Michael and his angels fought against the dragon, and the dragon and his angels fought back. But he was not strong enough, and they lost their place in heaven. The great dragon was hurled down—that ancient serpent, called the devil, or Satan, who leads the whole world astray. He was hurled to earth, and his angels with him.
>
> Revelation 12:7–9

The Good Guys

Before we start talking about the bad guys, let's make sure we understand the good. Again and again in the Bible, we see angels delivering messages from God, defending those who love him, conquering our enemies, and worshiping God at his throne.

The same is true today.

I often hear stories of dying people who saw an angel off in the corner waiting to accompany them to heaven. Or I hear of missionaries who were protected by "glowing men with swords" whom they couldn't see, but their attackers could.

One of my favorite stories is of a woman in Oregon who was

injured and stranded in the freezing wilderness for a week. No one believed she could have survived until she explained that after she prayed, two glowing figures of light appeared by her side each night and used their golden light to keep her warm. They never said a word and disappeared at daybreak each morning until she was found.

Now that's cool.

Unfortunately, there are also ...

The Bad Guys

According to the Bible, there are also real bad guys out there. What makes it worse is that at first, at least for us mortal types, it's often impossible to see the bad ones for what they really are. Extremely dangerous.

Maybe you've seen or heard of popular stories that portray fallen angels as dashing teenage boys who pursue human female love interests. They're shown to be supernatural beings who made the mistake of falling in love and must now pay for all time. In their world, God is a bully who punishes them eternally for one mistake. Your heart goes out to them, right?

The truth of the matter is, these fallen angels (about one-third of Heaven's population) embraced the evil of their leader, Satan, and rebelled against God. They were thrown out of Heaven and became demons. Something you definitely wouldn't want to take a moonlit stroll with. And their purpose for humans? One thing and one thing only. Like their boss, they want to steal, kill and destroy.

The problem is Satan and his demons don't walk around in red tights, with horns sprouting out of their heads, and carrying pitchforks.

So how do we tell the difference between angels and demons?

Angel Worship

First of all, there's real danger in thinking angels are something they're not. And it's especially dangerous when a natural and healthy awe of angels grows into full-fledged worship. The Bible is clear that angels are *not* to be worshiped.

Check out what happened when the apostle John tried to worship one: "I fell at his feet to worship him. But he said to me, 'Do not do that! I am a fellow servant with you and with your brothers and sisters who hold to the testimony of Jesus. Worship God!'" (Revelation 19:10).

And if you ever run into an angel who allows himself to be worshiped, watch out ... They'll use your awe to control, hurt, and destroy you, even to the point of possessing you. In other words, a good angel will always point you to God and his messages; a bad angel will point you to himself and the messages Satan wants you to hear.

My Encounter

As a young man just out of college, I received a phone call from a fellow who claimed he was in constant contact with angels. It would have been easy to dismiss him as a nutcase, except he was a psychic celebrity who used these "angels" to help the police solve crimes. (He told me that's how he got my telephone number—in a dream.)

During our conversation he told me the angels sometimes spoke through him, and he offered to let me speak to one. I thought, *Cool*, and quickly agreed.

Immediately, his voice changed—completely. It became stronger, deeper, and full of authority.

I was pretty excited and remember putting my hand over the mouthpiece and whispering to my wife, "I'm talking to an angel!"

Over the next couple of days, I had more conversations with the guy and several of his "angels." Was he faking it? I don't think so. Each entity that spoke through him was so unique, with its own voice and personality, that I was sure I was talking to several different beings.

Besides, they told me things about myself he couldn't have known except through supernatural means. For instance, they knew I was an aspiring writer. One of the voices assured me that I was going to be a successful author and that I was going to accomplish great things for God through my writing. Of course this was exactly what I *wanted* to hear. It's like the "angels" went out of their way to feed my pride and tantalize me with visions of glory. They kept flattering me to make me feel special.

They also offered to help me achieve this fame by working with me to write a book proclaiming the "deeper mysteries of God's love."

I began to grow uneasy.

I didn't know much about angels then, but I suspected that these beings didn't really have my best interest in mind. They were a bit too slick. And instead of encouraging me to grow in humility and love, they kept stirring up my pride and my desire for great success.

Finally, I decided to ask one of the beings a very important question. "Is Jesus Christ your Lord?" I asked.

"Absolutely!" he said.

But before I could breathe a sigh of relief, he added, "In fact, not only is he my Lord, he's also my brother."

I felt the hair on the back of my neck rise.

Why?

Because I remembered reading that Satan and his demons are driven by pride, a desire to be considered equal to God. Or, as God put it: "You said in your heart, 'I will ascend to the heavens;

I will raise my throne above the stars of God' … but you are brought down to the realm of the dead, to the depths of the pit" (Isaiah 14:13, 15).

Satan and his "angels" are so full of pride, they can't help themselves. If they see a chance to claim equality with God, they go for it.

I knew then that I wasn't dealing with angels but with demons. And once they realized I'd caught on to their scam, their attitude toward me changed completely.

At first, they tried to reason with me, wondering how I could be so "narrow-minded" and why I insisted on stubbornly clinging to my outdated beliefs in the Bible.

When I wouldn't give in, they started insulting me, saying I was stupid, calling me names, and using language that didn't fit into any holy angel vocabulary.

There's more to the story, which I'll tell you later. The point is, the beings speaking through this man were definitely not the good guys they claimed to be.

The Top Three Lies

Today, as I skim through some of the most popular books on angels, I see right away that I'm not the only one who has been lied to. When I check what these books say against the Bible, their half-truths become obvious—particularly the ones where:

- An angel seeks to draw attention to himself and not God.
- An angel gladly accepts the adoration of men and women.
- An angel appeals to our pride.
- An angel tells us that he will answer our prayers and give us what we desire.

- An angel leaves heaven because he has fallen in love with a human woman.
- An angel views God as less than all-powerful, good, and holy.

And yet the angels who are described in the pages of many of the bestselling books may do all of these things and more.

Basically, I see three major lies our enemy uses again and again. If you hear any of them coming from either a human or an angel, watch out:

1. Christ isn't the only Son of God.
2. There are many paths to God (which means Christ is a liar and his death on the cross wasn't necessary).
3. We all have within us the power to be like God.

None of these statements agree with the Bible *in any way.*

I've also noticed plenty of books and teachers that start off sounding like they believe in the Bible but then twist truths until they've got their audience heading down an entirely different path.

What Do the Bad Guys Want?

To answer that question, let me tell you about a couple of famous men who have listened to "angels."

The first is Muhammad, the founder of Islam. Did you know that the Islamic religion was founded on the teaching of an "angel"? According to Muhammad, it was the angel Gabriel who appeared to him and, among other things, taught him how Christians have things all mixed up … including the lie that Jesus didn't actually die on the cross.

As Christians, we know it wasn't Gabriel who appeared to Muhammad. But Muhammad believed it was, and so does the nearly 25 percent of the earth's population that follow his teachings.

Another man who listened to "angels" was Joseph Smith.

One night when he was twenty-five years old and thinking about what to do with his life, Smith reportedly was visited by the "angel" Moroni. Moroni said that he had come directly from the presence of God and that God had chosen young Smith to restore the Christian church, whose doctrines had been corrupted.

The "angel" directed Smith to a nearby hillside, where he allegedly dug up some ancient tablets covered with hieroglyphics. Smith carried the plates home and, even though he knew only English, began translating them. He worked for days on end, stopping only to eat or sleep, and never for very long. Finally, when he'd finished, Moroni appeared again and took the tablets back to heaven.

You may know that Joseph Smith was the founder of the Mormon religion and the work he "translated" was *The Book of Mormon*.

But there are some things about Smith you may not know …

For instance, before his encounter with the "angel," Smith allegedly had been involved in the occult. In fact, he'd developed a reputation as a "seer."

On May 3, an article in the *Chenango Union* newspaper of Norwich, New York, reported:

> In the year 1825, we often saw in that quiet hamlet Joseph Smith, Jr … (living with) the family of Deacon Isaiah Stowell … (who had) a monomaniacal impression to seek for hidden treasures, which he believed were hidden in the earth …
>
> Mr. Stowell … heard of the fame of … Joseph, who by the aid of a magic stone had become a famous seer of lost or hidden

> treasures.... He with the magic stone was at once transferred from his humble abode to the more pretentious mansion of Deacon Stowell.
>
> Here, in the estimation of the deacon, he confirmed his conceded powers as a seer, by means of the stone, which he placed in his hat. And by excluding the light from all other terrestrial things could see whatever he wished, even in the depths of the earth.[1]

This raises some interesting questions:

Did Joseph Smith's journeys into the occult pave the way for his encounter with the "angel" Moroni? Is this why the theology of the Mormon church contains elements found in occult writings?

For example, Mormons believe the God who rules over the earth is not Lord over the rest of the universe. They believe there are many planets with intelligent life on them and each of these planets is subject to a different god. In fact, they believe all human beings have within them *the potential to be like God.*

Sound familiar? Remember those top three lies?

Islam and Mormonism are two very different religions whose founders said they were influenced and guided by angels. And yet their teachings don't agree with each other, nor do they agree with the basic tenets of Christianity.

Ten Lies about Angels

Author Phil Phillips lists several lies about angels often found in occult literature[2]:

1. We should seek angels.

Many of today's popular "experts" on angels teach we should seek to have experiences with angels, and they give some ways to help make these possible. These ways include:

- Meditation.
- The chanting of mantras.
- Summoning the angels by name.

Let's look briefly at each of these practices.

First, meditation. There's a big difference between the meditation the Bible talks about and the meditation taught by today's Eastern and New Age teachers. Biblical meditation involves thinking of the Scriptures and *filling our minds with God*. Occult meditation involves *emptying our minds* to encounter supernatural creatures.

Next, the chanting of mantras. A mantra is a word repeated again and again in order to relax the body and enter an altered state of consciousness. Again, it involves emptying the mind and opening oneself up to dangerous supernatural encounters.

Then, the naming of angels. In her book, *Angels of Mercy*, Rosemary Ellen Guiley writes:

> We must discover names for our guardian angels if we wish them to manifest in their fullest magnitude. Name is an important ritual: it defines and it invests life, power and potential. Without names, we cannot call out to the higher planes; we cannot invoke or evoke the beings, forces, and energies into our own dimension.[3]

It's very interesting to me that some demonic rituals also summon demons by name.

The truth is that there is no power in the name of angels but only in the name of Jesus Christ.

2. Angels work miracles.

In *The Angel Book*, Karen Goldman says that "the angel in you can heal you in many ways. Angels can help to heal illness, poverty, anger, or despair. There is an abundance of pure healing energy, joy, creativity, and unwavering inner strength available for you at all times."[4]

Where is there room for God in all of this? Angels aren't in the miracle-making business. Miracles—including healing—are God's line of work, and he's still at it today. As a filmmaker who's made documentaries on missionaries, I have seen God do incredible things. Not man. Not angels. God.

3. All angels tell the truth.

We've already seen that this isn't the case. Angels aren't infallible. Remember that Satan himself was once a high-ranking angel, possibly an archangel, and yet Jesus said, "He was a murderer from the beginning, not holding to the truth, for there is no truth in him. When he lies, he speaks his native language, for he is a liar and the father of lies" (John 8:44).

4. When you're lost, angels desire to get inside your heart and lead you home.

This is very dangerous. *Demons* desire to get inside you, and when they do, it's called *possession*. Anyone who invites an angel "into his heart" is opening himself up to demonic control. The Bible tells us that it's the Holy Spirit's job to lead and guide us from within—the Holy Spirit and no other (Romans 8:6–11).

5. Angels can help us gain access to heaven.

Wrong. According to Jesus, "I am the way and the truth and the life. No one comes to the Father except through me" (John 14:6).

The *only* way we can get to heaven is to surrender control of our lives to Christ and accept the offer he made to pay for our sins when he died on the cross.

6. Human beings are able to become angels.

The Bible says we are two distinct creations. We aren't angels. Despite what the books, movies, or TV shows say, we'll *never* be angels. Scripture actually states that you and I will judge the angels (1 Corinthians 6:3).

7. Angels want to uncover our hidden goodness and make us like God.

The Bible does *not* teach that we have goodness in us apart from God or that we can become equal with him. Instead, we are a fallen, messed-up race, full of sin: "All have sinned and fall short of the glory of God" (Romans 3:23).

8. Angels are always reaching out to us.

The truth is, angels reach out to us only when God commands them to do so. They are his messengers—his servants—and their desire is to do his will.

9. Angels can be felt in every atom of creation.

Wrong again. As Phillips writes, "It is God who indwells every atom of creation by virtue of His creative power."[5]

10. Angels know what it's like to be human.

While it's true angels are created beings just as you and I, they do *not* know what it's like to be human. Popular literature may present angels with humanlike characteristics, but the Bible tells us that angels are created beings who are distinct from humans (Hebrews 1:14). They do not marry (Matthew 22:30) or have families. They are God's heavenly servants. And they will never know the joy of being saved from sin. Jesus died for humans, not angels. Angels know and love God deeply, but they can never sing "Amazing Grace" the way we can.

Summing Up

God's angels are watching over us every minute of the day, doing their best to keep us from harm. But I believe they reveal their true identity to us only when they're commanded to do so. Most of the time, they stay in the background, silent and invisible. Other times, we may encounter them and not even know we were in their presence: "Do not forget to show hospitality to strangers, for by so doing some people have shown hospitality to angels without knowing it" (Hebrews 13:2).

God's angels:

- Are his warriors and his messengers. They will never tell us anything contrary to his Word, the Bible.
- Never accept the praise or worship of men.
- Always seek to bring glory to God and Jesus Christ.
- Rejoice whenever someone puts his or her trust in Christ.
- Understand we're all powerless apart from God.
- Are ministering spirits who walk alongside the faithful, helping and encouraging those who are trying to live for God.
- Come to us to lead us to God.

Satan's angels:

- Are his warriors and his messengers and often claim to bring new and better truths to replace or update the Bible.
- Are quick to accept and even invite the praise and worship of men.

- Deny or downplay Christ's divinity.
- Say many paths lead to God.
- Tell us we have the power within us to become like God.
- Are anxious to get inside us to take control.
- Come to us to lead us away from God.

One Final Note

Usually, when people in the Bible encountered real angels, they were filled with terror and fear—often falling to the ground, covering their faces, and thinking they were going to die. The reason is pretty clear. Those angels just came from the awesome, holy presence of God.

When people who are involved in the occult meet their angels, they're often filled with warm fuzzies and told how great they are.

One is a demonstration of the awesome power of God as his angels come to share his message with humanity ... the other is a con artist trying to seduce a human with smooth words and cozy feelings.

Quite a difference.

---

1. W.D. Purple, *Chenango Union Newspaper*, Norwich, NY, May 3. 1877.
2. Phil Phillips, *Angels, Angels, Angels* (Lancaster, PA: Starburst Publishers, 1995). 103–107.
3. Rosemary Ellen Guiley, *Angels of Mercy* (New York: Pocket Books, 1991), 65.
4. Karen Goldman, *The Angel Book* (New York: Simon and Schuster, 1992), 85.
5. Phillips, 102.

3

Demons

Are they real?

You bet.

Who are they?

Most believe they're evil angels, set on tormenting humans any way they can.

There is some controversy, but many believe the evidence indicates they started out in heaven, just like all the other angels. But they were thrown out when they sided with Satan in his attempt to overthrow God. Over the centuries they haven't done much to improve themselves. In fact, they seem to have grown even more corrupt and evil. If there was ever a spark of goodness in them, it's long burned itself out.

Demons belong in hell. That's where they're going to spend eternity, and their one pleasure in life seems to be to take as many human souls with them as possible. Demons hate God. They hate me. And they hate you. They enjoy seeing us suffer and will do everything they possibly can to hurt us.

Why?

The best way to hurt God is to hurt his kids.

Sometimes demons decide the best way to inflict pain is to come disguised as angels—speaking of love, peace, and brotherhood—trying anything to entice us away from God. Later, when they know they have the upper hand in someone's life, they come in with fangs bared, snarling and growling like the monsters they are. Other times they're subtle, content to work through drug abuse, alcohol addiction, pornography, and other vices, never giving a hint that anything supernatural is going on until it's too late.

Nothing to Fear

Before we get further into the topic, there's one important thing we need to remember …

If you have given your life to Christ, you have *absolutely nothing to fear* from demons. In fact, if you're a Christian, *demons are afraid of you*! Why? Because they know God has given *you* authority over them. As usual, Jesus puts it best when he says, "In my name they will drive out demons" (Mark 16:17).

If Christ is the boss of your life, you have the right to act in his authority, and they *have* to obey you.

Yes, they're scary. They may make threats, and they may pull off some eerie "special effects." But if you belong to Jesus Christ, they have no choice but to eventually run when you confront them—like cockroaches in a dark room when you turn on the light.

On the other hand, remember that the name of Jesus in itself is not a magic wand anybody can use to take authority over a demon. If you're not living for Christ, you have no right to use his name or his authority. It's only when you're in a right relationship with him that you can fight demons and win. Otherwise, you might find yourself in the same embarrassing situation as the seven sons of Sceva:

> Some Jews who went around driving out evil spirits tried to invoke the name of the Lord Jesus over those who were demon-possessed. They would say, "In the name of Jesus whom Paul preaches, I command you to come out." Seven sons of Sceva, a Jewish chief priest, were doing this. One day the evil spirit answered them, "Jesus I know, and Paul I know about, but who are you?" Then the man who had the evil spirit jumped on them and overpowered them all. He gave them such a beating that they ran out of the house naked and bleeding.
>
> Acts 19:13–16

The sons of Sceva believed there was power in the name of Jesus, and they were right. The problem was they thought anybody had the right to use that power.

That's just one of the lies people believe when it comes to demons. There are even bigger ones ...

Lie Number One—Demons Aren't Real

Many "educated" people dismiss belief in demons as something outdated, a relic from a superstitious age.

But Jesus Christ himself believed in them, spoke about them, and exercised total authority over them. Here are just a few of many examples:

> Just then a man in their synagogue who was possessed by an impure spirit cried out, "What do you want with us, Jesus of Nazareth? Have you come to destroy us? I know who you are—the Holy One of God!"

> "Be quiet!" said Jesus sternly. "Come out of him!" The impure spirit shook the man violently and came out of him with a shriek.
>
> Mark 1:23–26

Also in the gospel of Mark, a man was inhabited by demons. The Bible says this man:

> ... lived in the tombs, and no one could bind him anymore, not even with a chain. For he had often been chained hand and foot, but he tore the chains apart and broke the irons on his feet. No one was strong enough to subdue him. Night and day among the tombs and in the hills he would cry out and cut himself with stones.
>
> Mark 5:3–5

When Jesus threw the demons out of the man, they went into a herd of pigs that was feeding nearby, and "the herd, about two thousand in number, rushed down the steep bank into the lake and were drowned" (Mark 5:13). After that the people of the area were afraid and begged Jesus to leave when "they saw the man who had been possessed by the legion of demons, sitting there, dressed and in his right mind" (Mark 5:15).

Again and again in the Gospels, we see that Jesus had absolute authority over demons. There was *never* an instance when they could withstand his power for even a second.

Mark also tells of a worried father who brought his demon-possessed son to Jesus' apostles for help, and they were unable to give it. But when Jesus arrived and commanded the demon to leave the child, "the spirit shrieked, convulsed him violently and came out. The boy looked so much like a corpse that many said, 'He's dead.' But Jesus took him by the hand and lifted him to his feet, and he stood up" (Mark 9:26–27).

The Bible goes on to say that "after Jesus had gone indoors, his disciples asked him privately, 'Why couldn't we drive it out?' He replied, 'This kind can come out only by prayer'" (Mark 9:28–29).

From these passages of Scripture and many others, we see that demons were very real and very active when Jesus walked the earth. And they're just as real and active today.

Lie Number Two—Demons Are Everywhere

Earlier I quoted C. S. Lewis, who said there are two very different but equally dangerous beliefs when it comes to demons. The first is to disbelieve in them or ignore them. The second is to give them more credit than they deserve and think about them too much.

A few years back some Christians were putting way too much emphasis on demons. It got to the point that one guy who was having car trouble asked me to cast the demons out of his engine. I passed, figuring a 60,000-mile tune-up would do a lot more for the car than an exorcism.

During that time some people taught we all had been invaded by demons, and there were gatherings where paper bags were handed out so people could vomit up the demons that were tormenting them.

It was all pretty weird. Pretty unhealthy. And very unnecessary.

Now the pendulum may have swung too far back in the opposite direction …

Then demons were blamed for all sorts of evil. Today many believe all evil happens only because man is messed up.

It's true—humans don't need demons to inspire them to new depths of evil. Or as Jesus said, "Out of the heart come evil thoughts—murder, adultery, sexual immorality, theft, false testimony, slander" (Matthew 15:19).

It's way too easy for someone to point his finger and say, "The devil made me do it," when he's really just following the instincts of his own evil heart.

On the other hand, demons are real. They will stop at nothing in their attempts to get us to cheat, lie, steal, kill, commit adultery, or do anything contrary to what God wants. They love it when we hurt other people. They love it when we hurt ourselves. But most of all they love it when we grieve God.

How Demons Operate

Most of the time demons aren't able to exert direct control over us. Instead they use guerrilla warfare, zinging us from the outside. They put various types of temptation in front of us. (Remember the Lord's Prayer? "Lead us not into temptation, but deliver us from the evil one," Matthew 6:13.) They hit us with impure thoughts. They try to get us to doubt God and distrust his Word. They tempt us to exercise the worst of ourselves—anger, selfishness, lust, violence, and cruelty.

But demons aren't content to direct things from the sidelines. They want to get in the middle of the action. If they can find a way, they'll get inside a person and try to take over his life. This is called *demonic possession.*

It's real, and it happens—not only in the Bible, but today as well.

My Encounter with Demons

What do you think of when you hear the word *demon*?

If you're a fan of old scary movies, you might think of Linda Blair, who starred as the demon-possessed, head-spinning teenager in the 1970s movie, *The Exorcist.*

You may remember her sitting in bed with her head spinning around, or her vomiting pea soup, or any of the other gruesome scenes.

The Exorcist—supposedly based on a real-life case of demon possession investigated by the Roman Catholic Church—was a blockbuster movie that got the whole world talking about demons. It was followed by a slew of copycat films, including *The Exorcism of Emily Rose* in 2005 and *The Last Exorcism* in 2010. But it was *The Exorcist* that got the whole demon-possession movie craze going.

As for me, I've never seen it.

Oh, I wanted to. I remember when it first came out; I drove to the theater and was standing across the street when I suddenly sensed that God didn't want me to go, that he didn't want me to see any film that glorified satanic power. As a result I was probably one of the few people in the country who missed Linda Blair's gross-out performance.

But it was God's grace that prevented me from seeing *The Exorcist.* Otherwise, I would have run the other way when, a few months later, I started receiving some very strange phone calls.

They came from the man I mentioned in the last chapter who spoke to "angels." Let's call him Jerry. As I said, I eventually realized there was something strange about his angels. One of the clues was Jerry continually begging them not to hurt me.

Hmmm … for heavenly creatures, they didn't seem all that loving.

Another thing that bothered me was how Jerry told me he always felt sick to his stomach right before one of the "angels" took over and spoke through him. As I mentioned before, Jerry had received public acclaim from the powers these entities gave him, and he was quite proud of that. But whatever was happening to him, it was far from a pleasant experience.

When I finally worked up the courage to ask one of Jerry's mysterious friends the all-important question, "Is Jesus Christ your Lord?" and he answered, "Not only is he my Lord ... he's my brother," I knew Jerry was in trouble. I didn't understand a whole lot about demons at the time, but I knew enough to know that anytime you come into contact with an entity that claims equality with Jesus Christ, you're not dealing with the good guys.

I wasn't sure how to handle the situation, never having come face-to-face—or telephone-to-telephone—with a demon before. I told Jerry he wasn't in contact with angels, but rather demons. He insisted I was wrong and worried that if I pushed the issue, he might lose his powers. I asked him to give me his address so I could come visit him in person and pray for him.

But he was just too frightened.

Soon a tug-of-war began inside Jerry. One minute I was talking to Jerry ... the next, one of the entities ... and then Jerry again. When the "angels" had control of Jerry, they insulted me and called me some blistering, X-rated names. When Jerry was in control, he kept begging them not to hurt me. Finally, twenty-four hours later, after he had called dozens of times, he gasped out his address. It sounded like it took every ounce of his strength to do so.

The next day I went to see Jerry, accompanied by a friend from my church. Before we went we bowed our heads in my car and confessed all of our sins to God, asking Jesus to forgive us. We knew we'd better be in a right relationship with God when we walked into Jerry's house. We didn't want to give the devil any ammunition to use against us.

I admit my heart was pounding when we walked up the short sidewalk to Jerry's neat, suburban house. (It definitely didn't look like the sort of place demons might be hanging out.) Still, I was worried about the battle waiting for us inside.

But the moment Jerry opened the door, all my fear vanished. He stood before me, a short, balding, fifty-year-old man who was terrified—a man who desperately wanted to be free. The moment I saw him, I was filled with such love that I instinctively threw my arms around him and hugged him.

It was the right thing to do. Later on he told me that at that moment he realized he could trust me.

We came into Jerry's living room, sat down, chitchatted for a while, and finally began to pray with him. As we prayed Jerry started to writhe and scream, but I knew it wasn't really Jerry who was in agony. We prayed for forty-five minutes. Some of the time Jerry sat still, and I began to think we were winning the battle. But the next moment he would go back to writhing and screaming.

When we sang worship songs, things really got nuts. The more worshipful the song, the louder he screamed and the more his body jerked and contorted.

After a while, when our prayers seemed to be losing steam, I decided to recite the Lord's Prayer. That really sent Jerry into a frenzy. He howled as if I were pouring acid on him.

At first I didn't understand what was going on. What was so different about the Lord's Prayer that it would cause these entities to react this way? Then it dawned on me. I was praying the Word of God. This was the same weapon Jesus himself used to fight Satan when they battled it out on the mountain of temptation.

No wonder the Bible tells us the Word of God is sharper than a two-edged sword.

I pulled out my Bible, turned to the Psalms, and began to read. The reaction was just the same. Screaming. Swearing. Howling. Gnashing teeth.

Finally my friend and I got down on our knees in front of Jerry, laid our hands on him, and began to pray that he be free of the creatures. The first two or three demons surfaced; we recognized them through their strange voices and facial expressions, and we easily threw them out in Jesus' name.

But others were more deeply entrenched in his life and didn't want to let go. When he was a little boy, a witch had helped him invite them inside so he could have "supernatural powers." As a result many of these demons had been with him since childhood. We prayed and prayed and prayed some more, but these stronger demons made it clear they weren't going to leave without a fight.

Now, as I said, my friend and I had never encountered demons before, and we were unsure of what to do. We didn't want the demons to hurt Jerry by throwing him on the ground, so we held him down tightly while we prayed for him. It was during this time another fellow came walking through the front door—Jerry's roommate. I'm sure we made quite a scene. For all he knew, we were a couple of burglars who'd been caught in the act. He could have ordered us to leave his friend alone. He could have threatened to call the police.

Instead, all he said was, "Hi, guys." He acted like it was the most natural thing in the world to see two big men holding little Jerry down like that. He went on into the kitchen, made himself a sandwich, and then left.

Later on Jerry asked him why he didn't try to stop us or at least ask us what we were doing.

"It was the oddest sensation," the man replied. "But there was something different about those guys. Were they … angels?"

"Angels … no. Why?"

"I'm not sure. I just knew I wasn't supposed to stop them."

Our session with Jerry went on for hours, as various demons

were brought to the surface and thrown out in Jesus' name. It was interesting that each had its own particular character trait. For example, one had very strong homosexual tendencies. He called himself "the Persian boy" and claimed to be a departed spirit who once had a homosexual relationship with Napoleon. He spoke in an effeminate male voice. While this demon was in control of Jerry, his body language changed completely. He crossed his legs in a feminine manner, spoke with a lisp, and seemed to be a completely different person. As soon as we had taken authority over the demon and removed him in Christ's name, Jerry was back to his old self.

Now before I go on, I want to make it clear that I do *not* believe homosexuality is caused by demons. I do believe that some demons may manifest homosexual behavior or tempt their victims into this particular sin ... just as they tempt others into any other sin. Demons show their presence in a variety of ways. The Bible tells us Jesus cast out demons that caused their victim to be deaf and mute. Does this mean all people who are deaf or who can't speak are inhabited by demons? Of course not. And yet I filmed a Sri Lankan man who experienced that very problem. Today he is a pastor with his speech and hearing completely restored.

The same mistake can be made about people who suffer from Dissociative Identity Disorder (formerly Multiple Personality Disorder). This is a legitimate psychological problem often brought about by severe trauma during childhood. People who suffer from it develop numerous and distinct personalities in order to cope. Unfortunately, many well-meaning Christians have done more damage than good by mistaking this disorder for demonic activity and trying to "cast the demons out." This is why prayer for discernment is *so vital* in these situations.

Because of Jerry's psychic powers (which he had received by

inviting the entities to come inside him), I knew we weren't dealing with some type of psychological disorder but rather with demonic creatures who had invaded his life.

It was late in the evening by the time we finished praying with Jerry. It had been a long day, and we were exhausted. By our best count, we had successfully encountered and removed twelve of the creatures, and as far as I could tell our time with Jerry had been a complete success. He seemed happy and relaxed, and he told us he couldn't remember when he had felt so peaceful.

But it didn't last.

The next night my wife and I were getting ready to go out for dinner when the phone rang.

"Bill?" Jerry sounded frightened. "There are still some here."

He was agitated and wanted me to come right away. But I had promised my wife a dinner out, and I wasn't about to break that promise. I told him I'd come the following afternoon.

Immediately, a haughty, sarcastic voice took over.

"We won't be here," it growled at me. "We're taking him to New York, and there's nothing you can do about it!"

"No way," I said. "You're not going to do that. By the power and authority of Jesus Christ, you cannot take Jerry off that property until three o'clock tomorrow afternoon."

Then I hung up, and we went on to dinner.

The next day my friend and I went back to Jerry's, and when we pulled up in front of his house, we were greeted by a strange sight. He was pacing back and forth in his yard, looking very much like a caged animal. Every once in a while, he tried to step onto the sidewalk, but he couldn't do it. He'd lift his leg in the air and lean forward, but it seemed as if an invisible barrier was stopping him.

"Bill!" he yelled. "I don't know what's going on here … but I can't leave my yard!"

He didn't know what was going on, but I did. It wasn't three o'clock yet. By my command in Christ's name, he couldn't leave his property until then. It was at that moment, more than ever, that I was struck by the absolute authority that belongs to those who believe in Jesus Christ.

We took Jerry to our church office, where some reinforcements joined us. There were several more demons lurking down deep in Jerry's soul, including one that tried to get him to jump from the upstairs window.

As evening approached, I was completely drained. I just wanted to go home and sleep. Two days of intense battle with demons had taken a toll on me so I was more than a little relieved when it appeared that we were down to the last demon. But that last one was holding on with both claws. It wasn't going to leave without a fight.

Suddenly, one of our pastors—a man who was reluctant to believe in much of the supernatural—had a mental picture of Jesus, standing off to the side, watching the proceedings. He told us later that Jesus slowly turned and glanced in Jerry's direction. At that exact moment Jerry opened his mouth and let out a shrill, bloodcurdling scream. By the time the scream had finished echoing up and down the halls of the church, the final demon was gone, and Jerry was free at last.

When our friend told us about his vision of Jesus, I shook my head in awe. Our Lord didn't even have to speak a word to beat the demon. All it took was a single glance.

I've heard some people say that God and Satan are adversaries—equal but opposite forces. No way. If I hadn't known it before, I learned that day that Satan is no adversary for God. He's nothing more than plaque on God's teeth.

For a more detailed telling of all that took place, check out my E-book, "Supernatural War."

If the subject of demons is new to you, you may have been startled by the events I've just recounted. And you may have some questions.

What Exactly Is Demonic Possession?

Possession is what happens when a demon or demons actually take up residence inside a human body. As I mentioned before, demons aren't content to merely harass us from the sidelines. If a demon sees a chance to enter into a man or woman's soul and take control, he'll do it.

Why do they want to do this?

First, it enables them to destroy a human being, and there's nothing they enjoy more.

Second, demons like to have a human body because it gives them a vehicle to carry out their dark plans.

Third, demons attempt to possess us because they enjoy the pleasures of the flesh. They have insatiable appetites for things like sex, alcohol, narcotics, and gambling. As a result they often steer their victims into addictions in these areas.

How Does It Happen?

As with Jerry, some people actually invite demons into their lives—a few because they believe they're opening themselves up to angels or spirit guides. In addition, those who are deeply involved in occult practices are putting themselves into greater danger of demonic possession. The same goes for those involved in drug use. In Deuteronomy 18:10 the Bible warns that God's anger will fall upon those who "practice sorcery." The root word for *sorcery* is *pharmakeia*, which means *drugs*. It's the root from which we get our modern words *pharmacy* and *pharmaceuticals*. It's not a coincidence that the Bible equates the use of illegal narcotics with sorcery. There are documented cases of excessive use of addictive drugs leading to demonic enslavement.

Michael Fishback is the former executive director of the Bakersfield, California Rescue Mission. He worked with the poor and homeless for more than two decades. He'll tell you that when he started out, he didn't think very much about demons. Like many Christians, he knew demons existed because the Bible talks about them, but he didn't think they were a real problem in today's world. Now he knows differently.

"I've seen so many things that can't be explained any other way," he says. "I've seen people who we couldn't help—at all—until we took authority in Jesus' name over the demonic influences in their lives."

Michael Fishback doesn't think all alcoholics or drug addicts are afflicted by demons. But he believes that some are, and these people can't be rehabilitated until they've been set free from demonic bondage. And again, discernment—asking God for wisdom, as well as talking to Christians with more experience in this area—is the key. It's important that we *not* look at every evil habit or practice as a case of demonic oppression or possession. Some of it is just good old-fashioned sin. So how can we tell?

Recognizing Possession

It's not always easy to tell whether a person is demon-possessed or suffering from some psychological ill. Is that guy controlled by demons, or is he suffering from schizophrenia? Is this woman a demoniac, or does she suffer from Dissociative Identity Disorder?

If we're confronted with a situation in which we suspect demonic involvement but aren't sure, the best thing we can do is ask God to reveal the truth to us. And he will, because if there's one person more concerned than we are about seeing demons' victims set free, it's our loving Father in heaven.

There is, however, one other surefire way I believe we can tell when we're dealing with demons: As my experience with Jerry showed, a person who is demon-possessed can't stand to listen to the Word of God, nor be in the presence of those who are worshiping the Lord.

Who Has the Authority to Cast Out Demons?

Anyone who has accepted Jesus Christ as their Savior and who is living in a good relationship with him has the power and authority to cast out demons in Jesus' name.

Having said that, I need to caution that going up against demons isn't always easy, and it must *not* be taken lightly. If you're not sure you're in a right relationship with God or if you have unconfessed sin in your life ... don't do it. Demons know what scares us, and they'll use it. They know where our weak spots are, and they'll hammer away at them. They'll taunt us and laugh at us and ask us who we are to think we can defeat them ... even though they know Christ has given us the power to do just that. I wouldn't recommend getting involved in this type of ministry if you're the least bit timid or squeamish.

A Strong Warning to Students

If you're a young person or a new Christian, *never* attempt to confront a demon unless you're accompanied by a pastor or someone who's mature and experienced in this area. And be sure to listen to them. Avoid anyone who's looking for the "thrill" of a supernatural encounter. Instead, find that man or woman who is thoughtful, wise, and godly.

How Can I Prevent Possession?

The very best way to keep demons out of our lives is not to open the door in the first place—and to stay close to God. Or, as the Bible says, "Submit yourselves, then, to God. Resist the devil, and he will flee from you. Come near to God and he will come near to you" (James 4:7–8).

Demons can't stand to be in the presence of God. It follows, then, that if you're walking closely with God through reading your Bible, going to church, praying, and worshiping, demons won't be all that thrilled to hang around you. They may try to bug you for a while, but not for long.

Deliverance Isn't Enough

Before we leave the topic of demons behind, I want to make one more thing clear. When a person is inhabited by demons, it's not enough to cast them out in Jesus' name. Unless that person begins living for God by sincerely asking Jesus to become their Lord and Savior, the demons will return at their first opportunity.

Jesus put it this way:

> "When an impure spirit comes out of a person, it goes through arid places seeking rest and does not find it. Then it says, 'I will return to the house I left.' When it arrives, it finds the house swept clean and put in order. Then it goes and takes seven other spirits more wicked than itself, and they go in and live there. And the final condition of that person is worse than the first."
>
> Luke 11:24–26

Despite the dramatic conclusion of a successful deliverance, it's important we understand that doesn't mean the battle is over. In her excellent book *Enticed by the Light,* Sharon Beekmann explains how demons will usually return to tempt and torment their ex-hosts over the next several months to years. We must stand beside a newly delivered believer, encouraging him not to give in to old patterns and to continually take authority over the voices until gradually they quit returning and trying to re-enter.

Let me repeat: *A successful deliverance is only the beginning of setting the new believer free.*

There's a lot more we could say about demons. We could give example after example of their evil nature and determination to destroy anyone who comes in contact with them.

But the most important thing to know is that they're absolutely powerless when facing the love and power of Jesus Christ. As long as we're in a right relationship with him, we have nothing at all to fear from hell.

4

Satanism

Look deep into the eyes of Sean Sellers, and tell me what you see ...

A normal young man. A guy you'd be friends with. Perhaps a surfer or the best skateboarder in the neighborhood.

Certainly not a cold-blooded killer.

And yet, in the middle of a quiet, ordinary night, Sean Sellers crept into his parents' bedroom and brutally murdered them.

He didn't do it because his parents were abusive—they weren't. Nor was it because there was friction in the family or because his parents didn't understand him.

He said he did it because he believed it would bring him honor and power from his "master."

Several weeks prior to the murder of his parents and the fatal shooting of a convenience store clerk earlier that same evening, Sean Sellers had dedicated his life to Satan.

Turn your attention now to America's heartland—the city of Keokuk, Iowa. No one would expect to find devil worship in this all-American community. That's why residents here were shocked when two young men tried to kill themselves as a result of their involvement in satanism. One young man survived. The other died.

Pearl, Mississippi also made headlines when a teenager there was arrested for killing his mother and a classmate, allegedly as the result of his involvement in a satanic group. He says now that the leaders of the group ordered him to carry out the killings, and he obeyed. People were left shaking their heads and saying, "This kind of thing can't happen here."

But it did.

What's going on? Why would anyone want to follow Satan down a road that leads to death, destruction, and hell?

As we search for the answers, let's travel to upstate New York to visit a friend of mine—a fellow by the name of David Berkowitz.

Talk with a Serial Killer

David makes you feel at ease the moment you meet him. He's a likable guy with a twinkle in his eye. In fact, the first time I met him, I was tempted to ask, "What's a nice guy like you doing in a place like this?"

You see, David Berkowitz is in prison and will stay there for the rest of his life. He's considered such a threat to society that when they locked him up, they threw away the key. Why? For a brief period in the mid-1970s, David Berkowitz terrorized New York City as the infamous "Son of Sam." That's how he signed letters to the New York City Police Department, where he taunted them and vowed to continue a bloody killing spree that was making newspaper headlines across America.

Before he was apprehended, Berkowitz was accused of

shooting thirteen people, seven of them to death. When he was finally caught and convicted, his sentence was "life without possibility of parole."

Shortly after Berkowitz was arrested, he confessed to the killings but said that he had been commanded to kill by a neighbor's dog—named Sam. That was why he had referred to himself as the "Son of Sam."

As you can imagine, Berkowitz was written off as just another lunatic—a very dangerous lunatic—and locked up.

But today, more than thirty-five years after his arrest, Berkowitz says that there was never any dog named Sam. He came up with that story simply because he was afraid to tell the truth. But in the years since his arrest and conviction, David Berkowitz has seriously surrendered his life to Christ, and because he's a committed Christian he wants to set the record straight regarding what really happened on the dark streets of New York City more than three decades ago.

He's not changing his story because he thinks it will help him. He believes he's serving a just sentence and knows that no matter what he does or says he'll never again be a free man. But he's serious about doing anything he can to prevent other young people from throwing their lives away as he did.

Was there a Sam? Yes. But Sam was not an evil canine who lived next door. Sam was the nickname of a demon summoned by the group of Satan worshipers to which Berkowitz belonged. He says it was the demon who ordered the murders, and he obeyed—partly out of fear, partly out of peer pressure, and partly because he lacked the freedom to *dis*obey.

A Familiar Story

David Berkowitz had the personality profile of most of the

young people who are attracted to Satan worship. Like Sean Sellers, he wasn't comfortable in school. He was bright, but his grades never reflected his intelligence. He didn't make friends easily and was something of a loner—an outcast. According to his website, David was a tormented soul from his youth. He was violent and disruptive in school. He craved darkness and would sit under his bed or in his closet with the lights off. He also struggled with thoughts of suicide.

David eventually dropped out of school, enlisted in the army, and served a tour in Vietnam. He says that when he came home to New York, his dreams were the same as any other young man. He wanted to find a nice girl, get married, settle down, and raise a family.

Instead, he found Satan.

David says his descent into murderous madness began when he met some people who seemed to take an interest in him. They were the type of guys he wanted to spend time with, and he was flattered by their interest. They had money to spend, and they liked having a good time.

These people accepted David without judgment and quickly won his friendship and loyalty. At first they spoke of mysteries and secret ceremonies. Since he had always felt drawn to darkness, he was intrigued. He had no idea his new friends had sworn their allegiance to Satan.

Finally, he was invited to attend one of their gatherings. There, it quickly became apparent what his new acquaintances were up to. David was repulsed by their worship of Satan, yes, but he was also fascinated and attracted. He should have run, but he didn't.

Over time he was drawn deeper and deeper into the satanic rituals. I don't believe it's necessary to discuss all of the things David participated in and experienced. Let me just say that according to what David told me, his acts grew more despicable and more violent.

Eventually, the group summoned the demon who used David Berkowitz to feed his hunger for human misery. The members of the group called the demon "Sam," which was short for the name he gave them when he'd first appeared.

Sam had stern words for Berkowitz and his fellow satanists. Satan was not satisfied with their puny sacrifices and empty talk about serving him. He wanted—no, commanded—them to prove their allegiance, and if they didn't obey, there would be hell on earth to pay. He wanted the ultimate sacrifice—a human life.

David Berkowitz knew Sam meant business. If he disobeyed orders, whether from Sam or other members of the group, he or his family would be killed. And so, armed with his .44 caliber revolver, David began prowling the streets of New York City, looking for victims. The "Son of Sam" became notorious from coast to coast, as the New York City Police Department tried desperately to find a way to prevent him from striking again.

Finally, they succeeded in capturing him. He was arrested and charged with seven counts of first-degree murder. The moment he was arrested, his friends disappeared. But he knew they were lurking nearby and that if he implicated them in any way, they would kill him or his family.

He was tried, convicted, and sentenced. He never said a word about the other members of the group—even though some, according to what David states now, had also been involved in the murders.

Narrow Escape from Hell

David Berkowitz probably would have been executed for his crimes, except that he committed them during a time when the death penalty wasn't legal in New York. Today he gives thanks for God's mercy that spared his life. He knows that if he had been executed, he would have gone straight to hell. But God had other plans for him, and it was in prison that he learned about the love of Christ from a fellow inmate. He renounced Satan, asked God's forgiveness for all his horrible deeds, and became a Christian committed to serving others.

I admit some people don't believe a word David Berkowitz says. They still write him off as a psychopath who's merely looking for a way to justify what he did. But I've spent hours talking with him in person, I've asked tough, skeptical questions, and I have come to believe him—not only because of his words, but because of his deeds. Today David Berkowitz leads Bible studies and prayer groups, works with mental patients, and raises money for overseas missions; one village chief in Africa has even named a child after him.

I've asked myself what reasons he could possibly have for inventing this story. He knows he's never going to get out of prison. He's certainly not trying to exonerate himself; he freely admits he committed some of the murders and takes full responsibility for his actions. As far as I can tell, there's only one reason why he decided to speak about what really happened in New York all those years ago. He wants to tell all who will listen about the saving power of Jesus Christ and warn them about the dangers of satanism.

Why Would Anyone Become a Satanist?

Despite strong warnings from people like David Berkowitz, many people in our society—especially the young—are attracted to Satan worship. They get involved with satanism for many reasons, but most of all because it gives them a sense of power or control.

As one teenager said, "The other kids know I'm into it, and they treat me with respect." Like David Berkowitz, this guy had trouble fitting in. He felt like an outcast, pushed around and picked on.

Some are attracted to satanism through the example of their

heroes—especially heroes from the darker music scene. This is nothing new. As early as the 1960s, the Rolling Stones promoted their image as "the bad boys of rock and roll" by giving two of their albums satanic titles: *Their Satanic Majesties Request* and *Goat's Head Soup.*

I certainly don't believe all metal music is dedicated to the devil or is necessarily dangerous. But I also think it's important to be wise when it comes to selecting the music we hear. Listening to lyrics full of violence, illicit sex, despair, and death isn't healthy because, like it or not, our minds, souls, and emotions really are influenced by what we feed them.

Researcher John Charles Cooper puts it this way:

> It is fanatical to believe that every youth who plays fantasy games or enjoys heavy metal rock music is into occultism, but young people found engaged in destructive occultism usually are involved in thrash metal.... The lyrics, dress, symbols and lifestyles of these ... performers make satanism attractive to many young people from a very early age. Join the sadistic lyrics and blatantly perverse sexuality of these rock bands to the intoxication of pot, alcohol or hard drugs, and you have very heavy conditioning that might well tip a teenager into antisocial behavior.[1]

As I've said, satanism in music is nothing new. Marilyn Manson, with his multimillion-selling album *Antichrist Superstar* is a typical example in a long line of rock musicians who have claimed allegiance to the devil. Some may be quite serious. Others pretend to be satanists because it makes them seem sinister and dangerous and helps sell CDs.

According to Bob and Gretchen Passantino, noted experts on satanism:

> Even the most explicitly satanic band, Slayer, denies its members actually practice satanism or believe in the demonic supernatural

their lyrics celebrate. King Diamond is the only widely popular metal musician to consider himself a serious, dedicated satanist, and Diamond carefully explains that he doesn't believe in the supernatural—only in natural forces beyond most humans' knowledge or control.[2]

The Passantinos also quote Diamond as saying:

"When I use the word *Satan*, it doesn't stand for a guy with horns. To me, that word means the powers of the unknown, the powers of darkness.... I don't believe in heaven and I don't believe in hell as a place with flames where people are burning and having eternal pain. I don't believe in that at all. I believe in a place I call 'beyond.'"[3]

Is he right? Are we merely living in a *Star Wars* type of universe, surrounded by "forces" that we can use either for good or evil? Or are musicians like Diamond, Slayer, Marilyn Manson, and the latest newcomers playing with forces they don't understand—forces that will eventually turn against them?

Religion of Deception

Satan also likes for us to accept the lie that there's no such thing as a personal embodiment of evil. He doesn't care so much whether we believe in him—he just wants to make sure we don't believe in God. He seems happy if he can get us to live in some moral never-never land, where everything is relative, where there's no such thing as absolute good or evil, and where all are free to follow their own desires.

He claims that God is a killjoy who only wants to stifle us and keep us from realizing our full potential. "Enjoy life," he says. "Have fun. Don't limit yourself." But can you imagine living in a world where everyone did exactly as he pleased? It's hard to mprehend the chaos that would result from such unbridled selfishness.

The Nine Satanic Statements:	What the Bible has to say in response:
1. Satan represents indulgence, instead of abstinence.	1. Offer your bodies as living sacrifices, holy and pleasing to God (Romans 12:1).
2. Satan represents vital existence, instead of spiritual pipe dreams.	2. I [Jesus] have come that they may have life, and have it to the full (John 10:10).
3. Satan represents undefiled wisdom, instead of hypocritical self-deceit.	3. The fear of the LORD is the beginning of knowledge, but fools despise wisdom and instruction (Proverbs 1:7).
4. Satan represents kindness to those who deserve it, instead of love wasted on ingrates.	4. Love your enemies, do good to those who hate you, bless those who curse you, pray for those who mistreat you (Luke 6:27–28).
5. Satan represents vengeance instead of turning the other cheek.	5. If someone slaps you on one cheek, turn to them the other also (Luke 6:29).
6. Satan represents responsibility to the responsible, instead of concern for psychic vampires.	6. Do good to all people (Galatians 6:10).
7. Satan represents man as just another animal, sometimes better, more often worse than those that walk on all fours, who, because of his "divine spiritual and intellectual development," has become the most vicious of all.	7. God created mankind in his own image (Genesis 1:27).
8. Satan represents all of the so-called sins, as they all lead to physical, mental, or emotional gratification.	8. The wages of sin is death (Romans 6:23).
9. Satan has been the best friend the church has ever had, as he has kept it in business all these years.[4]	9. Your enemy the devil prowls around like a roaring lion looking for someone to devour. Resist him, standing firm in the faith (1 Peter 5:8–9).

And yet this is exactly the kind of world satanists strive for. "Do what you will" is the cornerstone statement Satan has built his kingdom on.

The Church of Satan, founded by Anton LaVey, is built on selfishness and greed. Compare the nine core statements of the Satanic Church with what God has to tell us in the Bible:

It's easy to see the differences in philosophy between those who follow Satan and those who belong to God. It's also easy to imagine the different societies such philosophies would produce.

And just for the record, let me give a few other reasons why satanism is a lousy idea.

Satan Has *Already* Been Defeated

Satan has kicked up quite a bit of dust and caused a lot of trouble over the centuries, but he has zero chance to grab control from God. Anyone who believes that Satan is going to emerge victorious is operating under the false assumption that God and Satan are equals. This is far from the truth. It's true Satan and God are opposites in that God is pure goodness and Satan is pure evil—but in *no way* are they equals. Satan's opposite number would most likely be an archangel, such as Michael or Gabriel. Archangels are powerful, yes, but they're created beings just like you and me. If there were a battle for control of the universe, it would not be waged on an equal footing. If Satan were a fly, God would be an elephant. Actually, if Satan were an amoeba, God would be a hundred billion elephants. It's still an inaccurate analogy, but you get the picture.

Also, it's *not* true that Satan is the "dark lord" of the underworld or that he's going to be some sort of supreme ruler in hell. I don't even know where we got that idea. It certainly isn't what the Bible teaches. Satan is going to wind up in hell, yes, but he's not going to be the ruler there. He's only going to be an inmate.

Many Eastern religions teach that God and Satan have both existed forever, that they might be considered opposite sides of the same coin. Wrong again. Satan is a created being, the work of God's hand. But like his human counterparts, Satan was given free will to choose whether he would do good or evil, and he chose evil. His existence had a beginning, and it will have an end. His fate is already sealed. The Bible explains, "And the devil ... was thrown into the lake of burning sulfur ... and ... will be tormented day and night for ever and ever" (Revelation 20:10).

That doesn't sound like the sort of general I'd want to follow into battle.

Satan Always Plays into God's Hands

Romans 8:28 says that "in all things God works for the good of those who love him, who have been called according to his purpose." That doesn't mean Christians aren't going to go through trials and tribulations. All of us hit bad times. Jesus warned us that it would be that way: "In this world you will have trouble. But take heart! I have overcome the world" (John 16:33).

This means that if we belong to God, even when bad things happen to us we know that something good will come out of it. For Christians everything that happens to us will ultimately work to our good.

God is capable of taking everything Satan means for evil and turning it into good. In one sense you can't help but feel a little sorry for Satan when you see how hard he works to defeat God but then always winds up playing into God's hands.

Even when Satan thought he won the greatest victory, it became his worst defeat. I'm talking about the crucifixion of Christ. Satan thought he'd won the war. He must have been beside himself with joy when he saw Jesus nailed to the cross. He must have been delighted as he watched the Son of God slowly die in agony and thrilled when he saw the spear thrust into Jesus' side as proof that he was dead.

What Satan didn't know was that it was all part of God's plan to free us from the slavery of sin. Satan had done *exactly* what God wanted him to do. And Satan's chokehold on this planet was smashed when Jesus walked out of the tomb, alive, three days later.

Today, Satan is still constantly defeated by God. God allows Satan to test and challenge us, yes, but according to Paul, that's for three reasons:

1. To discipline and correct us.
2. To help us relate to others who will be suffering.
3. To make us as complete and mature as Jesus Christ.

I remember a story I heard about attempts to ship fresh North Atlantic cod from Boston to San Francisco during the 19th century. At that time the only way to ship the fish to the West Coast was to sail around the South American continent—a trip that took months. As you can imagine, the first attempts to prepare the cod in Boston and pack them in ice failed miserably. By the time they reached California, the fish weren't exactly fit for eating.

Next, the cod were placed in holding tanks full of water, shipped to California alive, and prepared there. The results weren't so great either. The fish didn't get much exercise during the trip, and as a result, they were pasty and tasteless.

Finally someone had an interesting idea.

"Why don't we put some catfish in with the cod?" Why? Because catfish are the natural enemy of cod. Sure enough, when a few catfish were placed in those tanks, the cod were always alert and swimming around. This time, when the fish reached San Francisco, they were in perfect shape.

You might say that Satan is nothing more than a catfish in

the water to ensure our spiritual muscles are kept firm and in good shape.

Satan Wants to Destroy Everyone

… even his own soldiers.

Where is David Berkowitz today? Serving life in prison.

Sean Sellers was executed on February 4, 1999, as punishment for his crimes.

It ought to be clear that Satan isn't the *least* bit interested in protecting his own. He's not interested in helping anybody, for any reason. Instead, he knows he's eventually going down, and he's determined to take as many with him as he can.

He may promise rewards, but he *never* delivers.

That's the way he's always been …

He promised Adam and Eve the knowledge of good and evil if they disobeyed God and ate the forbidden fruit. Instead, they received a death sentence.

He even tried to turn Jesus away from his mission by showing him the great kingdoms of the world and promising, "I will give you all their authority and splendor; it has been given to me, and I can give it to anyone I want to. If you worship me, it will all be yours" (Luke 4:6–7).

But Jesus saw through the scam and answered, "It is written: 'Worship the Lord your God and serve him only'" (Luke 4:8).

Satan tries to get people to obey him by making wild promises he'll never fulfill. But if he can't get people to obey him by sweet-talking them, he goes for the threats: "Obey me or I'll destroy you." That's what David Berkowitz feared. He was afraid he or his family would be destroyed if he didn't obey Satan.

David obeyed, and his life was destroyed anyway. When it comes to a partnership with Satan, nobody wins.

Satan Can't Touch Us If We Belong to Jesus

There are dozens of reasons why it doesn't pay to join Satan's team. But the final thing I want to do before we move on is remind you that unless he has God's permission, Satan can *never* harm those who belong to Christ.

That doesn't mean he won't try to make us think he's going to hurt us or won't try to scare us. But it's all smoke and mirrors with no reality. Without God's permission the worst he can do is simple, special-effect parlor tricks.

And even when he pulls those, all we have to do is remember our authority over him in the name of Jesus.

The Bible tells us that, as Christians, we have nothing to fear from the devil because "the one who is in you is greater than the one who is in the world" (1 John 4:4).

And the book of Hebrews tells us that Jesus died so that "by his death he might break the power of him who holds the power of death—that is, the devil—and free those who all their lives were held in slavery by their fear of death" (Hebrews 2:14–15).

The bottom line for all of us is this: If we belong to Christ, we have absolutely *nothing* to fear from Satan. He can bluster and threaten all he wants, but we are *always* secure in God's protective hands.

---

1. John Charles Cooper, *The Black Mask: Satanism in America Today* (Old Tappan, NJ: Fleming H. Revell, 1990), 77.
2. Bob and Gretchen Passantino, *When the Devil Dares Your Kids* (Ann Arbor, MI: Servant Publications, 1991), 117–18.
3. Passantino, 33.
4. Anton Szandor LaVey, *The Satanic Bible* (New York: Avon Books, 1969), 25.

5

UFOs

Denver, Colorado. Just past ten o'clock at night, Peggy Otis drove down a quiet residential street with her young granddaughter, Jennifer, asleep beside her.

Suddenly something in the sky attracted her attention. It was an airplane, apparently coming in for a landing at Denver International Airport.

Guess again.

It wasn't an airplane. It was way too low … and it was going to crash into the street right in front of her!

Peggy remembers that "sparks were being emitted from underneath it, and it suddenly came down so low that I thought it was going to smash the top of my car. I screamed at Jennifer to wake up and jumped out of the car. The craft was dome-shaped, and I could see someone moving inside it. We were terrified, thinking that it was going to crash into us."

It didn't crash into Peggy's car, nor did it fall into the street.

Instead, after lingering for a few scary moments, it simply floated away. But before it did, something even stranger happened.

Someone from the craft spoke to her. She didn't hear an audible voice, but the message was strong and clear: "Don't forget us."

That was all.

Later that evening Peggy told her husband what had happened, and he called the airport to see if anyone had reported seeing anything out of the ordinary. No one had. Mrs. Otis described the craft as making a noise like that of a garbage disposal and said that it came low enough that she could see people inside of it—and yet nobody else saw a thing.[1]

What was it that Peggy Otis saw that night in Denver? Whose voice did she hear?

Cochran County, Texas. The sheriff's department responded to an agitated call from a rancher who complained that "something" was killing his livestock. The rancher said things were so weird he couldn't explain them over the phone.

When the sheriff went to investigate, the rancher drove him to a spot a couple of miles from the house, where a circle about thirty feet in diameter had been pressed into a wheat field. And there, in the middle of the circle, was a dead cow that had been butchered with surgical precision. Its tongue had been removed, along with its navel. Apart from the tongue no other edible meat had been taken. Whoever had killed this animal wasn't interested in food, and they hadn't butchered it at that spot. There was no blood on the ground.

About a quarter of a mile away from the cow, the men found a dead steer lying in the middle of another large circle. It had been butchered in exactly the same way, but there was something different here. Within the circle itself, the wheat had been burned down to within four inches of the ground. The only explanation was that something very hot had come out of the sky and almost landed there—almost, but not quite—otherwise, the wheat would have been burned to the ground.

The sheriff's subsequent investigation turned up nothing further, except that several area residents reported seeing "strange lights" in the sky around the time the animals had been killed.[2]

What had happened in Cochran County, Texas … or in Denver, Colorado?

An Old Story that Keeps Getting Weirder

A businessman by the name of Kenneth Arnold first coined the term "flying saucers" back in 1947. Arnold was describing some weird-looking aircraft he had seen from the cockpit of his private airplane.

Over the next several years, thousands of people all over the world reported seeing other strange crafts maneuvering through our skies. Some were saucer-shaped, like the ones Arnold saw, some were cigar-shaped, and still others seemed almost jelly-like—blobs that had no clearly defined shape. All agreed they were like no other aircraft anyone had ever seen. They flew at speeds of several thousand miles per hour. Sometimes they hung almost dead still in the sky. Other times they shot up into the sky so fast they completely disappeared within seconds. They also made impossible ninety-degree turns and could stop in an instant.

In 1948, some claimed a flying saucer had crashed near Roswell, New Mexico and the Air Force had recovered bodies from the wreckage. The Air Force later issued an official statement saying that the crashed vehicle wasn't a spacecraft at all, but a harmless weather balloon. Many people didn't believe it. Some still don't.

By the mid-1950s several books had been written accusing the Air Force of trying to keep the American people in the dark about what was happening. Most of the authors felt something otherworldly (and most likely sinister) was going on, and the Air Force was keeping a lid on it—probably because the truth was too frightening for us to handle.

These authors also believed that "something big" was just around the corner. They felt the secrecy was going to end, and we'd all know the truth about unidentified flying objects by 1959 or 1960 at the latest. More than likely, they said, the government was going to announce that we had made contact with advanced beings from a nearby planet, probably Venus or Mars.

It didn't happen.

Here we are, sixty years later, and we don't know any more about flying saucers than we did when Kenneth Arnold reportedly saw the first. We don't know where they come from. We don't know what they're made of. We don't know why or if they're really coming here.

But one thing we do know: the reports won't go away. Thousands of sightings are reported to authorities every year. UFO investigator J. Allen Hynek says that between Arnold's day and 1990, there were a minimum of 700,000 sightings in the United States alone and millions worldwide.[3] And according to the Mutual UFO Network, in 2011 the number of UFO sightings increased by 67 percent over the previous three years, with an average of 500 reported sightings each month.[4]

Over the years the sightings have changed. Now strange circles are supposedly being imprinted into grain fields here and in Europe. There are also numerous reports of cattle mutilations. And more interesting, the sightings have become much more personal.

Millions of people throughout the world claim that they have made contact with aliens from deep space—many of them against their will. In 1990, UFO researcher Clifford Wilson said he believed there were 50,000 cases of these "close encounters of the third kind" on record.[5] Since then, there have been thousands more reports of alien abductions.

Who Are They, and What Do They Want?

Some alien abductees report having medical experiments performed on them. They say the aliens seem especially interested in the human reproduction system. Others tell of being chased and taken aboard spacecraft against their will. Some say they'll never again be able to sleep without a light on.

Of course all of this is disturbing. But what's even more disturbing is that a growing number of people have been "given messages" to deliver on behalf of the aliens. Most of the messages have to do with love, peace, and learning to live in harmony with each other. On the surface that all sounds very good.

But underneath there's a secondary message that sounds strangely familiar—often something along these lines:

You are gods. Learn to unlock the power within you. Throw off the shackles of your narrow-minded religions (especially Christianity) and join us in experiencing your divine godhead.

The message is identical to much of the occult teachings delivered by the fallen angels we discussed in chapter two.

What's even more coincidental is that thousands of people throughout the world have claimed to be making contact with beings from space through meditation, channeling, automatic writing, and similar methods that are *all* considered occultist in nature. It seems strange for any "advanced civilization" to use these questionable and unreliable means of delivering important messages to us. But then again, the messages we're receiving from these "aliens" aren't exactly trustworthy.

Going back to the early days of close encounters, we almost always find that the UFOnauts claimed to be from Venus, Mars, or one of the other nearby planets. But since science now indicates there are no advanced civilizations on nearby worlds, the aliens have simply changed their story. Now they come from Zeta Reticuli, Wolf 24, Alpha Centauri, or some other distant region of the universe—areas that, coincidentally enough, we can't check out.

Even if they did come from somewhere in the neighborhood of Alpha Centauri, which is the nearest star, it would take them 80,000 years to get here by conventional means. Even traveling at the speed of light, it would take hundreds or even thousands of years to get here from most points in space. This means they would have to travel faster than the speed of light, which, according to the laws of physics, is absolutely impossible.

And Since We're Talking Science ...

Astrophysicist Hugh Ross, founder and president of the organization Reason to Believe, has spent years analyzing hundreds of UFO sightings. Dr. Ross states that people are definitely seeing something unusual. Even though 95 percent of all sightings are eventually explained as cases of mistaken identity, there are still far too many unexplained sightings to write the whole thing off as weather balloons, swamp gas, and such.

But having said that, Hugh Ross also believes that the 5 percent of legitimate UFOs can't possibly be physical objects. If they were, they would have to follow the laws of physics—and they don't.

Here are ten reasons from Hugh Ross as to why UFOs are not physical objects:[6]

1. No physical artifacts have been recovered.

Despite numerous rumors of crashes, captures, and other close encounters with unidentified flying objects, Dr. Ross says that to date, there's not one documented case of physical evidence being collected. If UFOs were physical objects, fifty-plus years of visiting Earth most certainly would have resulted in some sort of physical evidence being left behind.

2. Some UFOs have been seen but couldn't be photographed. Others have been photographed even though nothing could be seen.

Dr. Ross says the same thing has happened with radar. On occasion UFOs have been plainly seen hovering in the sky, but radar screens at nearby airports or military installations don't show a thing. At other times radar has picked up strong signals from craft moving through the sky, but nothing has been seen.

It's *impossible* for physical objects to behave in this way.

3. UFOs don't create sonic booms.

If you've ever lived near an air force base, you know the thunderous boom that occurs when a supersonic jet breaks the sound barrier. It shakes the house and occasionally it breaks windows. And yet UFOs travel in and out of our atmosphere at speeds many times faster than sound, and they do it in complete silence. According to the laws of physics, that's impossible.

4. UFOs have been seen making ninety-degree turns at speeds estimated in excess of eighteen thousand miles per hour.

Remember the last time someone took a corner too fast and you were thrown to the side of the car? Or they hit the brakes and you flew forward? Try that at eighteen thousand miles per hour!

Solid aircraft simply couldn't survive such turns, nor could any creature inside of them. A person who was inside a spacecraft that did make a turn like that would have to be scraped off the walls with a spatula. A solid ball of steel can't survive a right-angle turn at only five thousand miles per hour.

Nothing can survive such a turn at the speed these craft are reported to be moving.

5. UFOs have been observed to change shape, size, and color at random.

A solid object can't change instantaneously from an oval to a circle to a square and back to an oval. Liquid, yes. Gas, yes. But a solid, no. And yet UFOs have been observed to do all of this and more.

6. UFOs have been performing a number of other maneuvers that are physically impossible.

For example, on one occasion two UFOs were reportedly seen traveling at a high rate of speed directly at each other. Observers on the ground braced themselves for a disastrous crash, but it never came. Instead, the two objects simply merged into one larger "craft." After a few minutes they separated again. During another sighting a large UFO suddenly split into five smaller objects, which then came back together. UFOs have also disappeared and then reappeared, and they have disintegrated only to "reintegrate" a few moments later as if nothing had happened.

When two cars collide head-on, even if they're only going twenty miles an hour, the result can be devastating. How is it, then, that objects traveling hundreds of times that speed can merge without causing so much as a dent in each other? It can't happen—not to physical objects. And yet, according to dozens of witness reports, it does.

7. No communication between UFOs has ever been detected.

If "flying saucers" were interplanetary spacecraft, we almost certainly would have intercepted communications between them. But even though we've had our ears turned to the skies for decades, we haven't heard a thing. Instead, these craft speed through our skies in complete silence.

This brings up another interesting point. If these objects really came from deep space, their arrival would have been recorded by some of the world's top observatories. And yet, even though there are dozens of extremely high-powered telescopes in observatories around the world, none of them has ever recorded an image of a craft approaching the earth from space. Nobody sees them coming. Then, all of a sudden, they're here.

8. Some UFOs have been seen shooting out "finite" beams of light.

In other words, they send out a beam of light that goes out so far and just stops. But light simply doesn't behave that way. It keeps going, either until a solid object, such as a wall, stops it, or, if there's no object to stop it, until its energy is dissipated. According to Dr. Ross, this is just another of the many things UFOs do that aren't compatible with the rules that govern our physical universe.

9. Although thousands of photographs of UFOs have been taken over the years, none are of high quality.

Have you ever seen a clear photo of a UFO? I haven't. They're almost always blurred. My first inclination would be to believe the blurring was intentional on the part of the photographer who was trying to pull a fast one. But then some of these objects photographed have been seen by hundreds of people, so that rules out deception. And yet, if the UFOs were real, physical, solid objects, they wouldn't blur this way.

Think about the photos you've seen of the space shuttle. Were any of those blurry? More than likely, they were crisp, clear, and sharp, even though the shuttle was traveling at a very high rate of speed. Ross says that physical objects simply do not blur the way UFOs do when they're photographed. The fault doesn't lie with the photographs or their photographers, but with the objects themselves. They appear blurry on film because they *are* blurry. They aren't real in the sense that they aren't solid, physical objects.

10. Magnetic field measurements don't concur with magnetic disturbances that are taking place.

UFOs have reportedly caused disruption of earth-bound communications. They have made car engines stall, induced power blackouts, caused clocks and watches to stop dead in their tracks, and so on. And yet when people have tried to measure the electromagnetic energy that has caused this to happen, it's simply not there. As Dr. Ross says, something "real" is taking place, but it's not physical. If it were, we could measure it.

Where Do UFOs Really Come From?

But if the UFOs aren't physical, what are they? Why are they here? And where have they come from?

The "space aliens," whoever they may be, seem very religious and zealous in spreading their views. When they "communicate" (through séances, automatic handwriting, psychics, and abductees) they often urge us earthlings to open our hearts to the universe through meditation and other mystical practices. They seem quite comfortable with Eastern-style religious practices and very much in agreement with many of the components of New Age teachings.

The only religion they seem to disdain is Christianity, which they label as "narrow-minded and divisive." They have no problem throwing Christ's name around, but they have zero tolerance when he's mentioned as the only begotten Son of God who died on the cross to save us from our sins.

Again, it's highly unlikely the UFOs zipping through our skies are interplanetary spacecraft. All indications are that they represent a supernatural phenomenon of a far different kind.

Years ago, UFO investigator John Keel made a creepy discovery about one particular alien:

Thousands of mediums, psychics, and UFO contactees have been receiving mountains of messages from "Ashtar." Mr. Ashtar represents himself as a leader in the great intergalactic councils that hold regular meetings on Jupiter, Venus, Saturn, and many planets known to us. But Ashtar is not a new arrival. Variations of this name, such as Astaroth, Ashar, Asharoth, etc., appear in demonological literature throughout history, both in the Orient and the Occident. Mr. Ashtar has been around a very long time, posing as assorted gods and demons, and now, in the modern phase, as another glorious spaceman.[7]

Who is Ashtar?

He's actually mentioned in the Bible as one of the pagan gods the Israelites were commanded not to worship when they entered the Promised Land. God told his people that when they came into Canaan, they were to "break down their altars, smash their sacred stones and burn their *Asherah* poles in the fire" (Deuteronomy 12:3, emphasis mine). (Asherah is another name for Ashtar.)

That alone ought to be enough to make us wonder who's really behind the whole UFO phenomenon.

Jacques Vallée is one of the world's most noted UFO investigators. He holds a master's degree in astrophysics and a Ph.D. in computer science. He has addressed the United Nations on the topic of UFOs and was the inspiration for the character Lacombe in the film *Close Encounters of the Third Kind.*

During the years Dr. Vallée has been involved in UFO research, he has carefully analyzed hundreds of the most baffling sightings and written several books on the subject.

When he first began investigating UFOs, he wasn't convinced there was anything mysterious or sinister about them. Most of the sightings, he figured, would be fairly easy to explain as a simple misinterpretation of data. If UFOs were real physical objects, the most plausible explanation would be that they came from other planets.

Today Dr. Vallée is convinced UFOs are real. But he's no longer certain they come from planets.

He writes that during his years of researching UFOs, "I had become aware of some pretty shady business behind the apparently harmless antics of the contactee groups. Now I wanted to focus my attention on the problem at hand: the question of who was doing all this and what their designs on us might be."[8]

I don't know anything about Dr. Vallée's spiritual beliefs. If he believes in God, he's not outspoken about it. But in everything he does, he tries to be the consummate scientist—completely open-minded, judging every bit of evidence on its own merits. And yet in his book *Messengers of Deception*, he has proposed the idea that UFOs are part of a master plan to sweep away the earth's old social order, including all existing religions, to make room for the new.

Over the years he has interviewed dozens of people who claim to have made contact with or received messages from beings they believed came from other worlds. Almost universally these people talked about the importance of establishing a unified, one-world government that would put an end to wars and rumors of wars. They're excited about the potential of a new economic system in which money will be eliminated and all people everywhere will share equally in the planet's worth. And they talk about a new worldwide religion that would reveal the true nature of the universe and free us from all our old, outmoded notions of eternal truth. In many ways it sounds exactly like the social and political climate of the one-world government spoken of in Revelation, the last book of the Bible.

Dr. Jacques Vallée isn't the only one who believes that aliens—or whoever they are—are trying to bring about a change in our society. Dr. Allen Hynek, whose credentials include his tenure as chairman of the astronomy department of Northwestern University, wrote:

> I have the impression that the UFOs are announcing a change that is coming soon in our scientific paradigms. I am very much afraid that the UFOs are related to psychic phenomena.
>
> Certainly the phenomenon has psychic aspects. I don't talk about them very much because to a general audience the words "psychic" and "occult" have bad overtones. They say, "Aw, it's all crazy." But the fact is that there are psychic things; for instance, UFOs seem to materialize and dematerialize. There are people who've had UFO experiences who've claimed to have developed psychic ability. There have been reported healings in close encounters and there have been reported cases of precognition, where people had foreknowledge or forewarning that they were going to see something. There has been a change of outlook, a change of philosophy of persons' lives. Now you see, those are rather tricky things to talk about openly, but it's there.[9]

Ronald Story, in his book *Guardians of the Universe?* adds, "It can be said, with certainty, that a 'conditioning process' is taking place, which is either directly or indirectly related to the UFO phenomenon."[10]

Occult-Like Experiences

It seems obvious that many people are ready and willing to believe any message that comes from space. After all, they figure, if these beings are so technologically advanced that they can travel billions of miles through space, it only makes sense that they're also far advanced when it comes to things like philosophy, religion, and personal morality.

That's the type of thinking that sent Whitley Strieber's book *Communion* rocketing to the top of the bestseller lists for several weeks in 1987. It told of Strieber's encounters with strange beings who often invaded his home in the middle of the night. Prior to these uninvited visits, he sometimes saw lights in the sky, so Strieber naturally assumed his strange visitors came from outer space. Wherever they came from, their visits always left him feeling depressed, angry, and worried about the safety of his wife and young son.

Initially, Strieber didn't remember anything about these intruders. He only knew he was experiencing panic attacks and felt troubled by bits and pieces of strange memories that made no sense—such as looking up into huge, almond-shaped eyes as he lay frightened in his bed. It was only through hypnosis that he remembered the full scope of what had been happening to him.

To Strieber's amazement he received hundreds of letters from readers saying they had undergone similar experiences. They told him he was reporting their own stories in exacting detail, right down to the almond-shaped eyes of the intruders.

Certainly, Whitley Strieber's stories about strange beings from outer space invading his home in the middle of the night are scary. But there's something even more troublesome. In *Transformation,* his follow-up to *Communion,* Strieber writes, "Maybe the visitors are gods. Maybe they created us."[11]

He goes on to say that one of the creatures "seemed almost angelic to me, so pure and so full of knowledge."[12]

When Strieber asked the creatures why they were here, they responded that they had come to "recycle souls."[13]

Over time, as Whitley Strieber's relationship with his strange "friends" deepened, so did his foray into the world of the occult. He had out-of-body experiences and visited with his long-dead father during one of those incidents. He became involved in shamanism, which he describes as "the oldest of all human religious traditions," and Wicca (which we will look at in depth later).

It's not surprising Strieber's encounter with "aliens" led him into the world of the occult. Dr. Hugh Ross has interviewed many people who claim to have been abducted by aliens, and he says he found that every one of them had been involved in the occult prior to their abduction.

There's simply no way we can reasonably deny the connection between the occult and UFO encounters.

Strieber has come to believe the appearance of his "visitors" has a strong connection to ancient—non-Christian—religions. He writes, "We have a life in another form—and it is on that level of reality that the visitors are primarily present."[14]

To any student of the occult, the most frightening of Strieber's comments is this:

> What is interesting to me now is how to develop effective techniques to call them [the visitors] into one's life and make use of what they have to offer … The most effective technique seems to be simply to open oneself, asking for what one needs the most without placing any conditions at all on what they might be.[15]

But if I open myself up to one of these beings, who am I really inviting into my life?

Are the creatures who come in UFOs mankind's saviors, as they claim to be? Do they really want to lead us to an era of peace and enlightenment?

Unfortunately, when the facts are closely examined, they speak for themselves. We're simply talking about old deceptions wearing new clothes. Not natural, but *super*natural; not extraterrestrial, but extra*dimensional*. It's the same old story—demonic entities finding new and improved ways to deceive, control, and torment.

---

1. Ruth Montgomery, *Aliens Among Us* (New York: G.P Putnam and Sons, 1985), 44-46.
2. Dr. Jacques Vallée, *Messengers of Deception* (Berkley, CA: And/Or Press, 1979), 85.
3. Quoted by Dr. Hugh Ross in the audiotape *ETs and UFOs* (Pasadena, CA: Reasons to Believe, 1990).
4. Email from Mutual UFO Network (MUFON) president, Clifford Clift, received on 10/15/2011: "Yes, MUFON has averaged 500 sighting reports per month this past year. In fact, we had 1013 sighting reports the month of August and 723 for the month of September."
5. Ross audiotape.
6. Ross audiotape.
7. John A. Keel, *UFOs: Operation Trojan Horse* (New York: G.P Putnam and Sons, 1970), 230.
8. Vallée, 137.
9. Ronald Story, *Guardians of the Universe?* (New York: St. Martin's Press, 1980), 149-150.
10. Story, 150.
11. Whitley Strieber, *Transformation* (New York: William Morrow, 1988), 7.
12. Strieber, 73.
13. Strieber, 198.
14. Strieber, 201.
15. Strieber, 236.

6

Communicating with the Dead

Fifteen-year-old Rhonda lived with her parents and older brother in a pleasant, middle-class neighborhood. She got good grades in school, was a member of the pep squad, and liked to hang at the mall, checking out the latest fashions and, of course, the boys.

All of that changed when her mom became ill. Even though her mother grew weaker and sicker, Rhonda refused to believe it. Three months later, at age thirty eight, her mom died.

Rhonda wanted more than her pastor's assurances that "Mom was in heaven and they'd be able to see each other again someday." She needed her right then. She would have done anything to hear her mother's voice—even if it meant hearing her mom nag her to clean up her room. Rhonda cried a lot. She didn't do her homework and no longer wanted to hang out with her friends.

Then one of them introduced her to the Ouija board.

Rhonda was skeptical at first when her friend suggested she could use the board to contact her mother "in heaven." Rhonda didn't know much about the Ouija board, and had always thought it was just a stupid kid's toy. But because she desperately wanted to talk to her mother, she decided to give it a try.

As her friend sat across from her, Rhonda rested her fingers on the plastic pointer and asked her mother's spirit to speak to her. The answer was immediate. The pointer began flying all over the board, spelling out messages from Rhonda's mom.

I've missed you so much!

Please don't cry for me; I'm happy here.

And so on.

Tears of joy rolled down Rhonda's cheeks as she and her mother chatted happily together about things that were important to them. It was such a comfort to know that she hadn't lost her mother after all.

The next day Rhonda couldn't wait to get home from school to talk with her mother again. The day after that she didn't even go to school.

As time went by the pattern intensified. Rhonda spent more and more time with her mother and less and less time with anyone else. At first her dad, lost in his own grief, didn't realize his daughter was withdrawing from life. But then he noticed the phone had stopped ringing and Rhonda's friends began leaving her alone. She had turned their invitations down so many times they stopped trying. He did receive calls from his daughter's teachers, who were concerned that Rhonda's grades were slipping. She was missing quite a bit of school, and when she did come, she spent most of the time by herself.

Meanwhile, still speaking through the Ouija board, Rhonda's mother didn't seem the least bit concerned her daughter's life was falling apart. Mom never asked how Rhonda's grades were coming along, never expressed a desire that her daughter should go out with her friends and enjoy herself. She didn't for a moment suggest that "a girl your age ought to spend more time with the living than with the dead."

Instead, she led her daughter deeper and deeper into the world of the supernatural. She introduced her to a number of her "friends" from the spirit world, talked with her about developing her "psychic powers," and brought "spirit guides" into her life.

I'd like to tell you that Rhonda's story has a happy ending—but I can't. The last time I saw her, she was gaunt, hollow-eyed, seemingly lost to this world. That was almost twenty years ago. Since then I've lost touch with her.

I think about her sometimes, and with those thoughts come a sadness and anger. I pray for her and hope she has found her way back to "reality," but I have no way of knowing for sure.

Rhonda was *never* in contact with her mother's departed spirit. She was talking to someone who knew her very well, someone who also knew her mother very well, but whoever it was, it was *not* her mother.

Now let's see if I can back up that statement.

The Ouija Board

What does the Ouija board look like? It's a flat, smooth board with letters and numbers on it, along with the words *Yes*, *No*, *Hello,* and *Good-bye.* The "players," usually two people who sit across the board from each other, place their hands lightly on a planchette, or pointer, which moves around the board, landing momentarily on letters and numbers to spell out answers to whatever questions are asked.

These boards have been around for a long, long time—some scholars say since at least six hundred years before Christ was born. Today the board is marketed as a toy. You can find Ouija boards on the shelves of toy stores, sitting alongside board games such as Monopoly and Life. Yet, as Rhonda's experience shows, the Ouija board isn't a toy.

Some experts dismiss the Ouija board as a fraud. Other psychologists who have studied it believe the pointer is moved across the board through the power of the subconscious mind. In other words, the person who is using the board is asking questions with his conscious mind and answering them with his subconscious. In extreme cases they believe this can result in a psychotic break and even in schizophrenia. Although this may occasionally be the case, my research and personal experience doesn't hesitate to place this "toy" in an even more dangerous category. I tend to agree with occult expert Edmond Gruss who says, "The content of the message often goes beyond that which can be reasonably explained as something from the conscious or subconscious mind of the operator." He goes on to say:

> The board has been subjected to tests which support supernatural intervention. The testing of the board was presented in an article by Sir William Barrett, in the September 1914 *Proceedings of the American Society for Psychical Research* (pp. 381–394). The Barrett report indicated that the board worked efficiently with the operators blindfolded, the board's alphabet rearranged and its surface hidden from the sight of those working it. It worked with such speed and accuracy under these tests that Barrett concluded: "Reviewing the results as a whole I am convinced of their supernormal character, and that we have here an exhibition of some intelligent, disincarnate agency mingling with the personality of one or more of the sitters and guiding their muscular movements."[1]

Many who have studied the Ouija board believe it is a means of communicating with voices from beyond. Here's what God has to say about that: "Let no one be found among you who … practices divination or sorcery, interprets omens, engages in witchcraft, or casts spells, or who is a medium or spiritist or who consults the dead. Anyone who does these things is detestable to the LORD" (Deuteronomy 18:10–12).

Pretty strong words. But why? Why is God so angry at this practice?

Desire to Deceive

We've already seen there are beings who are anxious and ready to communicate with us any time we're willing to open our minds to them. Sometimes they present themselves as angels; other times, as beings from other planets; and on still other occasions, as the *disembodied* spirits of loved ones who have died.

But I believe these voices "whispering in the wind" come from none of these places.

It's more likely they're the voices of demons anxious to lead us away from the truth … whose ultimate aim is to bring us into supernatural bondage. (If you haven't checked out chapter three, be sure to give it a read.) They seem to know just about everything there is to know about us, and they're very clever at using that information to convince us of their authenticity and win our confidence.

The fact they know so much about us doesn't surprise me. Demons make it a point to learn as much about us as possible. They're always watching us, looking for vulnerabilities and weaknesses so they can attack and bring us down. After all, they're trying to win a war.

And because of this, people who play with the Ouija board sometimes pay a very high price for their involvement. Gruss writes:

> The many cases of "possession" after a period of Ouija Board use also support the claim that supernatural contact is made through the board. Psychics and parapsychologists have received letters from hundreds of people who have experienced "possession" (an invasion of their personalities). Rev. Donald Page, a well-known clairvoyant and exorcist of the Christian Spiritualist Church, is reported as saying that most of his "possession" cases "are people who have used the Ouija Board," and that "this is one of the easiest and quickest ways to become possessed."[2]

My own experience with the Ouija board was short. It lasted less than an hour, but I think it says something very important about the power behind the device.

I was in junior high school when a friend brought his Ouija board to school. We spent some time playing with it during lunch, and it was working! The pointer flew all over the place answering our questions. I thought it was pretty cool, so I asked my friend if I could borrow the board.

That evening I asked my dad if he'd like to check it out with me. He didn't know much about Ouija boards either, but said that he'd give it a shot. We sat down at the dining room table to try it out, but we couldn't get it to respond. Instead of answering our questions, as it had done so quickly at school, the pointer simply sat there. It didn't move at all. Needless to say, I was more than a little disappointed.

It wasn't until the next day my mom told me she had been afraid of that board the moment I brought it through the door. She didn't want it in her house, and so the entire time my dad and I had been playing with it, she had been in the next room praying for our protection. That's why the board wouldn't work. God's power was there in a special way, and whatever forces were responsible for the board's operation couldn't get anywhere near us.

I'm not alone in thinking Ouija boards are dangerous. In his book *Channeling,* author Jon Klimo, who mostly takes an unbiblical view of communication with spirits and other entities and insists on the generally positive value of such experiences, writes:

> In the most comprehensive study to date, *Ouija: The Most Dangerous Game,* Stoker Hunt writes, "Because of the intimate nature of the information revealed, the Ouija Board is incredibly seductive. . . ." Hunt presents a sobering gallery of cases in which individuals reportedly relinquished personal judgment, lost control, even killed loved ones, under the direction of invisible guides of the Ouija Board. "In early stages of obsession or possession, the victim becomes increasingly reliant on the Ouija Board. He craves more and more revelations."
>
> Psychic authority Susy Smith agrees. "Warn people away from the Ouija Board ... until you have learned to be fully protected."[3]

The Rise of Spiritualism

Attempting to communicate with the dead is nothing new. It's been going on for thousands of years, as shown by the passage I quoted earlier from Deuteronomy. But the modern American "spiritualist" movement sprang from the alleged experiences of two sisters in 1848.

Margaret and Kate Fox were fourteen and twelve when their family moved into a small house in the town of Hydesville, New York. The family later reported they got very little sleep during the first three months in their new home. They were kept awake by various rapping and banging noises that seemed to come from somewhere inside the walls.

The family decided to try to communicate with whomever—or whatever—was making the noises. Mrs. Fox asked the entity if it knew the ages of her seven children. It quickly responded by correctly rapping out the ages of all of them, including a three-year-old who had died.

Mrs. Fox then asked, "Is this a human being that answers my questions correctly?"

There was no response.

"Is it a spirit? If it is, make two raps."

She wrote, "Two sounds were given as soon as the request was made."

Eventually the "spirit" identified itself as a peddler named Charles B. Rosna, who said he had been murdered in the house.

Before long the fame of the Fox family—and especially Margaret and Kate, who seemed to be the center of this spiritual activity—had spread throughout the region. The girls eventually began to give public performances where messages "from the dead" were given to the audience through means of the rapping, banging noises.

In their book *The Afterlife*, psychic investigators Jenny Randles and Peter Hough write:

> The press loved this new sensation. In 1849 the girls gave their first public performance in Rochester, then toured other towns in the eastern states. It was like a contagion. Other mediums joined the throng—the mainstay of this fledgling religion. Before long "spirit rapping" had spread across the entire United States, then over to Europe and Britain. This was the generation of Spiritualism—a movement built around the psychic abilities of two teenage girls.[4]

(Interestingly enough, rapping continues to be a significant feature of "supernatural communication." Whitley Strieber, the author of *Communion*, writes about attending a ceremony in which he and his friends heard loud rapping noises, which they assumed were produced by unseen entities.)

In 1851 three professors from Buffalo University investigated the Fox sisters, including their younger sister Leah, who had become a significant part of the story. They concluded the rapping sounds were a fraud. But these conclusions didn't diminish the sisters' popularity. Among their many fans was Sir Arthur Conan Doyle, creator of Sherlock Holmes, who became a convinced spiritualist and spent the last dozen years of his life deeply involved in the occult.

As for the sisters, their involvement in spiritualism didn't have a happy ending. Jon Klimo writes:

> All three Fox sisters married, some more than once; all, to varying degrees, sought refuge in alcohol. Margaret became an alcoholic. Thirty years after it had all begun, their relationships with each other had badly deteriorated. Leah had turned Catholic and was trying to take custody of Kate's two children. Margaret, who had sided with Kate, published a letter in the New York *Tribune*, in which she severed her ties with Spiritualism and claimed the whole thing had been a fraud. To get back at Leah, Kate joined Margaret in this confession. A year later, Margaret completely reversed herself, saying that the initial fraud exposé was done for money, under the influence of anti-Spiritualists. But the damage had been done, and it was ample ammunition for the press and disbelievers. Shortly thereafter, within three years of one another, all three sisters died.[5]

Despite the sad ending to the Fox sisters' story, Randles and Hough write that during the second half of the nineteenth century, spiritualism experienced tremendous growth:

> Spiritualism embraced other phenomena beyond spirit rapping. Telekinesis—the paranormal movement of objects, including furniture—was the most common. Occasionally, hands formed out of a substance called ectoplasm were seen manipulating objects. Indeed, entire entities were observed to be formed

> from such material, entities that were able to converse with those present.
>
> There were also "direct voice" mediums. Here, the disembodied voice of the deceased could be heard in the séance room. Musical instruments would play themselves and levitate around the sitters. "Spirit guides" became the vogue, too. Usually the deceased spirits of children or Indians, they took control of the medium. Whilst the medium was in a trance, the guide would take over the body and make use of the vocal cords. Many of the systems of communication with the afterlife developed then are still used by mediums today, although they tend to be less theatrical.[6]

Today, some mediums claim to have the ability to help solve murders by communicating with the victims after death. Others have become famous for advising celebrities. Still others have had TV shows based on their lives and experiences. Each of these psychics offers the same thing—the hope of reconnecting with a loved one who has died.[7]

Do I believe these individuals all have legitimate, supernatural experiences?

For the most part … *no.*

I believe most mediums are like slick salespersons, making a buck by exploiting another's grief. It's interesting to note that the world-renowned magician Harry Houdini spent a great deal of time proving the fakery of many of the spiritualists of his day. In fact he promised his wife that when he died, if there were any possible way to communicate with her, he would do it. The two of them arranged a special code known only to them. Interestingly enough, after Houdini died, his widow *never received a single message* that led her to believe her husband was attempting to communicate with her.

But even though I believe most spiritualists are fakes, the warning in Deuteronomy still stands. This is a very dangerous area and one that demonic forces are all too happy to exploit.

Randles and Hough try very hard to be objective in their investigation of the afterlife, but they write that spiritualism grew because "the dawning technological age caused many people to turn away from Christianity toward a religion more suited to the times. Christianity seemed antiquated in an age where things needed to be tested and evaluated on evidence—not just accepted as some 'whimsical' belief."[8]

There it is again—"Christianity is old and outdated. It's time to make way for the new." And yet Jesus himself said, "Heaven and earth will pass away, but my words will never pass away" (Matthew 24:35).

It seems to me that we're faced with a choice. Do we accept the words of entities who claim to be the spirits of dead loved ones … or do we accept the words of Jesus Christ?

Ben Alexander faced this choice. Alexander was once a prominent British medium but now heads up a Christian organization called Exposing Satan's Power Ministries. Alexander was a member of the Christian Spiritualist Church, which attempted to merge Christianity and occult practices. In many ways the church services were the same as any Bible-believing congregation—hymn singing, preaching, reading of the Scriptures, and even communion.

But every gathering also featured a séance, led by Alexander or another accomplished medium.

The church taught that Jesus Christ was the greatest spirit medium who ever lived and pointed to the Bible's account of his "transfiguration" as proof. This was the event where Moses and Elijah suddenly appeared with Jesus and he talked to them (see Matthew 17:1–5).

What Alexander and the others in his church failed to understand was that this was a one-time experience in which *God* was making clear that Jesus' authority is greater than Moses' or that of any of the other prophets.

As Alexander continued reading the Bible, he became troubled by Scripture that didn't fit with the beliefs and practices of his church. He was especially bothered by passages like these:

- Do not turn to mediums or seek out spiritists, for you will be defiled by them. I am the Lord your God (Leviticus 19:31).
- A man or woman who is a medium or spiritist among you must be put to death. You are to stone them; their blood will be on their own heads (Leviticus 20:27).
- When someone tells you to consult mediums and spiritists, who whisper and mutter, should not a people inquire of their God? Why consult the dead on behalf of the living? (Isaiah 8:19).

As God began stirring his heart, Ben Alexander became convinced he'd never really been in contact with the spirits of departed loved ones. The beings who spoke through him were clever mimics. Their performances were very convincing, but Alexander was certain that was all they were—performances.

He says that he could sense the displeasure of his spirit guides whenever he tried to spend time reading the Bible. He remembers that on one occasion an unseen force ripped the Bible out of his hands and threw it across the room. Another time, the pages started to spin rapidly, then be ripped out and tossed into the air. Instead of trying to explain away the Bible's prohibitions against communicating with the dead, Alexander's spirits were openly showing anger and contempt toward the Bible.

Eventually Alexander surrendered himself to Christ. He decided he needed to make a public statement of his new faith and follow Christ's command to be baptized.

The spirits were *really angry* then. In fact, on one occasion, he found a threatening message, written by a finger, on his car's fogged windshield: "We'll be waiting for you on the other side. We'll get you then."

But for all their bluster, the spirits never bothered Alexander again. He's convinced God is protecting him, and he's not worried at all about what awaits him "on the other side." He knows that when he dies, he will go to be with Jesus. Today he also knows why the Bible warns against attempting to communicate with the dead: It's opening yourself up to the possibility of invasion by sinister forces.

Following his conversion to Christianity, Alexander moved to the United States, where he built a successful ministry. Now in his nineties, he still lectures about the dangers of involvement in the occult. Years ago he occasionally traveled back to London where he tried to share the gospel with some of his remaining medium friends. Unfortunately he found that most of them were still bewildered by his "defection" and saw no reason to change their beliefs.

Ben Alexander's story adds an exclamation point to the fact that there is *no way* to reconcile what the Bible teaches with the practice of communicating with the dead.

A Ghost Named Philip

It all started when several members of the Toronto Society for Psychical Research wanted to see if they could *create their own ghost* and get it to show itself to them. They decided the ghost's name would be Philip and he had lived and died in seventeenth-century England. They even hired a writer to put together a fictional biography and asked him to make the account as heroic and romantic as possible. An artist was also commissioned to produce Philip's portrait. Following this, the members of the group were asked to learn everything they could about this fictional character, after which they would attempt to contact him on "the other side."

They tried for several months to communicate with Philip, without receiving so much as a whisper in reply. No surprise there—Philip had never existed. But as it turned out, that didn't matter.

One night, as the members of the group sat around a table calling out, "Hello, Philip!" something decided to make its presence known. A number of sharp raps sounded from somewhere inside the table.

In subsequent gatherings it didn't take much coaxing to get "Philip" to reappear. He quickly answered questions from the group by rapping on the table. He never contradicted what had been written about him, although members of the group reported he occasionally added details of his own. Sometimes the group would sing to Philip, and when they did, he joined in by bouncing the table up and down.

Finally Philip was introduced to the world through a television program, taped in front of a live audience at Toronto City Television studios. Traditional knowledge says that ghosts love the dark, but Philip wasn't the least bit bothered by television cameras and bright lights. When the show's moderator introduced him, he responded in the usual way—by rapping loudly on the table. And then the table began bouncing and bumping around on the stage.

For the next several minutes, Philip politely answered questions from several panelists and even members of the studio audience. He only fell silent when a member of the group that had "created" him challenged his existence.

"We only made you up, you know," he said.

With that, Philip stopped talking. It was only after members of the Toronto group redoubled their efforts to believe in him that Philip agreed to make a curtain call.[9]

This story brings up some intriguing questions: Who was Philip? Was he merely a product of the energy of the human mind? Or was his appearance the result of demonic activity? Had some demon, tricked into believing that Philip was a real person, decided to use Philip as a means of getting his own message across? Interesting questions. But whatever our conclusion, it doesn't negate God's severe warning in Deuteronomy: "Let no one be found among you who … is a medium or a spiritist or who consults the dead. Anyone who does these things is detestable to the Lord" (Deuteronomy 18:10–12).

Automatic Writing

Another way spirits of the dead supposedly communicate with the living is through what is known as "automatic writing." This involves holding a pen or pencil loosely in your hand and letting "the spirits" move it across the paper.

Some experts say that almost anyone who is willing to yield himself to the spirits can learn to be adept at automatic writing. All it takes is the ability to relax, empty yourself of conscious thought (sound familiar?), and allow the spirits to speak through you.

As you can imagine, the same dangers associated with Ouija

boards are also connected to automatic writing. Those who believe it's actually the power of the subconscious mind that takes control warn that a psychotic break and mental illness can result. Dr. J.B. Rhine, a Duke University psychologist who spent many years investigating occult phenomena, dismissed automatic writing as spontaneous "motor automatisms" and believed it was caused by inner conflicts, repressions, and obsessions that came to the surface during the process.[10] This may be true in some cases, but automatic writing does involve opening oneself up to the possibility of invasion by supernatural forces.

And many of the messages received through automatic writing are in exact agreement with messages being passed on through spirit mediums, "angelic" visitors, and beings who supposedly come from outer space. Again and again, Christ is hailed as a great teacher, but *never* as Savior. Frequently, people who engage in automatic handwriting are urged to unlock the power that lies within them. And they are told the afterworld is a peaceful, happy place for everyone, regardless of what has been done or believed in this life. In other words, we're told we might as well chuck most of the Bible, because what it says really doesn't matter.

Test the Spirits

Today, more than ever before, distinct voices are trying to get our attention. So it's vitally important to know how to tell a legitimate spiritual message from a counterfeit.

Author Phil Phillips in *Angels, Angels, Angels* gives these five very practical scriptural methods to "test the spirits."[11] He writes that an authentic messenger from God:

1. Proclaims and never denies that Jesus is God's Son and that he came to earth in fleshly form.
2. Always exalts Jesus Christ and points toward his atonement for sin, which he made when he died on the cross.
3. Never encourages divination or occult practices.
4. Never contradicts Scripture or dismisses its importance.
5. Never undermines the majesty, glory, or holiness of almighty God, King of the universe.

Good advice ... and perfectly in line with what the apostle John wrote:

> Dear friends, do not believe every spirit, but test the spirits to see whether they are from God, because many false prophets have gone out into the world. This is how you can recognize the Spirit of God: Every spirit that acknowledges that Jesus Christ has come in the flesh is from God, but every spirit that does not acknowledge Jesus is not from God. This is the spirit of the antichrist, which you have heard is coming and even now is already in the world.
>
> 1 John 4:1–3

There are many reasons why people may try to communicate with the dead. It's a difficult thing to lose a loved one, and like Rhonda, whose story I told at the beginning of this chapter, the bereaved may long for reassurance that their loved ones are happy "on the other side." But as we've seen, attempting to communicate with the dead is forbidden by God because it opens a door for Satan to deceive us.

Yes, according to the Bible, life does go on beyond the grave. For those who belong to Jesus, a wonderful time of reunion will take place in heaven. But until the time has come to join your departed loved ones there, the best things you can do are turn to the Lord for comfort, content yourself with wonderful memories of your loved ones, rest assured that they're safe, secure, and well in God's hands, and know that you will see them again someday.

---

1. Edmund Gruss, *Cults and the Age of Aquarius*, as quoted by Josh McDowell and Don Stewart in *Understanding the Occult (*Nashville: Thomas Nelson Publishers, 1992), 86.
2. Gruss, 96.
3. Jon Klimo, *Channeling* (Los Angeles: Jeremy P. Tarcher, Inc., 1987), 198.
4. Jenny Randles and Peter Hough, *The Afterlife* (New York: Berkley Books, 1993), 46.
5. Klimo, 99.
6. Randles and Hough, 47.
7. See *Primetime Nightline: Beyond*, aired 8/17/2011. In this discussion about psychic power, three psychics were featured: Dr. Gary Swartz; Rebecca Rosen, psychic to the stars, and Allison Dubois, on whose life the TV show *The Medium* was based.
8. Randles and Hough, 49.
9. Lynn Picknett, *Flights of Fancy* (New York: Ballantine Books, 1987), 173-176.
10. Randles and Hough, 79.
11. Phillips, 296-303.

7

Ghosts

A 2005 CBS Poll reveals that nearly half of Americans believe in ghosts.[1] A 2007 AP poll said 23 percent claim to have seen, heard, or felt the presence of a ghost at one time or another.[2] These are ordinary people who came face-to-face with something they didn't understand and didn't seek. They weren't trying to contact the spirits of the dead. It just happened.

Strangely enough, nearly one-third of people who say they have had an encounter with a ghost also say they are "doubters" when it comes to believing in life after death.[3] They know they've brushed up against something really weird, but they don't buy the notion it was a disembodied human spirit.

Does life go on beyond physical death?

The Bible clearly says the soul is eternal and we will either spend that eternity in God's presence or forever separated from him. Still, is this a valid reason for us to believe that so-called ghosts or apparitions are evidence of survival of the human soul?

If not, what are they?

The Ghost and the Video Game

Larry and Susan were thrilled when they were finally able to buy a house after more than ten years of living in an apartment. The house, in a suburb of Pittsburgh, wasn't a mansion, but it was twice the size of their apartment, and it was great to have some room for their boys, Jason, eight, and Derek, four.

One of the things Larry liked about the house was the finished basement, which he planned to convert into a rec room. The boys liked the basement too, and from the day the family moved in they spent a lot of time in there, playing and watching television.

The boys also started talking about the friend they'd met in the basement. They called him "the old man." Sometimes Larry would hear his boys laughing and carrying on down there, and when he asked, "What are you guys up to?" they'd tell him that "the old man" was telling funny stories.

Jason was in school, so he quickly made friends in the new neighborhood. But Derek spent a lot of time by himself. Larry decided to help fill the lonely hours by buying his son a video game system. He put it in the basement, still in its box, and told Derek he'd set it up for him over the weekend.

The next morning, as he was getting ready for work, he heard Derek's laughter floating up from the basement. He heard something else too: the beeps and blasts of the video game in action. When he went downstairs, he found Derek happily playing the game.

"Son? Who set this all up for you?" he asked.

"I did it myself," came the answer.

"You did?" It didn't seem like the type of thing a four year old could do.

"Well … not *all* by myself. The old man showed me how to do it."

More than a little unnerved, Larry called his office, told them he'd be coming in late that morning, and went to see the real estate agent who had sold him the house. He told the agent all about his boys' encounter with "the old man" and asked if there was anything about the house he ought to know.

After a long moment's hesitation, the agent finally said, "Your house used to belong to a man named Johnson. He was in his late seventies when he died."

"And?"

The real estate agent swallowed hard before continuing. "I didn't want to tell you this … but … he hanged himself. In the basement."

That's the story the way Larry tells it. He also says he thought about selling the house, but after he and his wife discussed it, they decided to stay. They loved the house, so they made the decision to share it with the strange entity, whoever or whatever it is, and strive for peaceful coexistence.

As far as I know, the arrangement is working out. They're not worried about any harm coming to them because they belong to Jesus Christ, and they know there is no spiritual power in the universe greater than him and his love. And yet, there's a very serious question here …

What exactly is going on in that house and in other similar houses around the world? My first inclination is to look for and believe in natural explanations, to pass the stories off as tall tales for those with overactive imaginations. Still, belief in ghosts has been around for thousands of years.

Chapter 14 of Matthew tells what happened when Jesus came to the disciples by walking on the water:

> Shortly before dawn Jesus went out to them, walking on the lake. When the disciples saw him walking on the lake, they were terrified. "It's a ghost," they said, and cried out in fear.
>
> But Jesus immediately said to them: "Take courage! It is I. Don't be afraid."
>
> Matthew 14:25–27

Some of the disciples had a similar reaction when Jesus appeared to them after his resurrection:

> While they were still talking about this, Jesus himself stood among them and said to them, "Peace be with you."
>
> They were startled and frightened, thinking they saw a ghost. He said to them, "Why are you troubled, and why do doubts rise in your minds? Look at my hands and my feet. It is I myself! Touch me and see; a ghost does not have flesh and bones as you see I have."
>
> Luke 24:36–39

Jesus didn't berate them for being superstitious. He didn't say, "You ought to know there's no such thing as a ghost." This isn't exactly an endorsement to believe in some sort of supernatural manifestation, but it's interesting that Jesus felt no need to address the issue.

It would seem that, in some way, ghosts exist. But, again, are they the spirits of the departed?

I don't think so.

I believe the evidence points to a number of different explanations, some very simple and others quite complex.

Can We Really Believe Our Eyes?

Some experts who have studied ghosts and haunted houses have come to the conclusion that many such experiences occur *only* in the eyes and ears of the beholder. In other words, they're a realistic type of hallucination.

Paranormal investigators Jenny Randles and Peter Hough write that ghostly manifestations may sometimes "have their roots in optical illusions or anomalies of perception. The will to believe can often provide its own persuasive evidence."[4]

Among other evidence to support this conclusion, they cite the story of Ruth, a woman who reported she was often visited by the "ghost" of her father. What made this so unusual, compared to other ghost stories, was that her father *was very much alive* at the time.

With the help of psychiatrist Morton Schatzman, Ruth was eventually able to control her ability to "create" realistic hallucinations. She had learned how to conjure up three-dimensional images of other people, and she sometimes had trouble telling the difference between her hallucinations and real people who were present.

In one experiment Ruth was asked to create an image of her father and get "him" to stand in front of some flashing lights, which were timed to interact with her brain rhythms. Ruth's brain activity was then measured to determine if she could see the lights through the image of her father. The experiment revealed that Ruth didn't see the flashing lights at all! It was as if her father really were standing in front of them. The ghost wasn't real, but it was real enough to block her vision.

Randles and Hough conclude, "These tests show that the brain is capable of 'seeing' something that is not there in such a realistic way that it can fool certain perceptual responses....

There is reason to suspect that apparitions could at least at times be very vivid hallucinations."[5]

Further experiments have shown that between 4 to 8 percent of us are "fantasy-prone." These people have a difficult time distinguishing dreams from reality and may have hallucinations that seem to be 100 percent real.[6]

There's no way of knowing for sure how many ghostly sightings have such logical explanations. But if 95 percent of all UFO sightings can be explained as a misinterpretation of data (as stated in chapter five), it's likely that a substantial number of hauntings are the result of similar misinterpretations.

Other hauntings seem to be related directly to a desire to believe.

In the early 1970s a British researcher named Frank Smyth decided to make up a ghost story, present it as real, and see if there was any response. He fabricated a story about the ghost of a clergyman who haunted a house in London, and had it published in a magazine. His story included the address of the house for those who might be inclined to check out the story for themselves.

Over the next few years, he received numerous reports from people who claimed to have seen the ghost. Some described the apparition in vivid detail, right down to his clerical collar.

When Smyth revealed that the story was phony, he was flooded with letters from people who insisted he was wrong. They were convinced they had really seen the clergyman's ghost, and nothing was going to make them believe differently. One such letter-writer insisted that Smyth only thought he made up the story, but that he had actually written it while under the influence of a real ghost.[7]

Big Business

Many other ghostly appearances and hauntings seem to be the result of plain, old-fashioned greed. There's plenty of money to be made in the ghost business.

Most people love a mystery. We like to be scared as long as there's no real danger involved. That's why so many of us enjoy roller coasters, scary movies, and the chill that creeps down our spines when we hear "true stories" about events that have taken place in haunted houses—houses like the one featured in the film *The Amityville Horror* … and its many sequels. The story is fairly typical:

1. A gruesome mass murder takes place in the house.
2. An unsuspecting family buys the house, not knowing its terrible history.
3. When they move in, they are subjected to all sorts of attacks by the malevolent entities that haunt the house—things like overpowering stenches, swarms of flies, sudden drops in temperature, green slime appearing on doors and walls, and objects flying through the air.

The family's ordeal became the subject of a best-selling book and several movies … but not everyone agrees on the details. Some people who were said to be present when strange, awful things took place have now said they saw nothing out of the ordinary.

It's been alleged that the family who bought the house was in desperate need of money. And it has also been reported that the attorney for the man who was charged with the murders that took place in the house met with the family in an attempt to get them to state publicly that the house was haunted.

Why?

The allegation is that he hoped to convince a jury that his client was innocent because he had been under the control of evil supernatural forces when he committed the murders—the same forces, you see, that were now tormenting the new owners of the house.[8]

What really happened in Amityville? Many believe that, beyond four gruesome murders, not much of anything.

Another Story

The same can be said of one of the most famous haunted houses in the world, England's Borley Rectory, which was built in 1863. The first sighting of a ghost there reportedly took place in 1885. In 1900, the four daughters of Henry Bull, who built the rectory, reported seeing the ghost of a nun walking the grounds.

One of the most famous occurrences in Borley was the rearrangement of several heavy coffins in the building's crypt. The coffins reportedly weighed several hundred pounds apiece, but some strange force kept rearranging them as if they were a bunch of dominos.

The building's reputation was enhanced during one six-month period in 1927 when a dozen clergymen and their wives visited the rectory with an eye toward taking up residence there. All of them decided against it, for various reasons, which reportedly included strange noises and other spooky happenings.

Finally, the Reverend Guy Eric Smith and his wife moved into the house. They managed to stay for nine months. During that time they reported often hearing footsteps and voices echoing through the house when there was no one else there. They also told of seeing a ghostly horse-drawn carriage coming up the driveway, and were especially troubled by a doorbell that kept ringing when there was no one at the door. Eventually, they said that they'd had enough and moved out.

At least that's the way the story goes. But …

The fact is, Borley Rectory owed much of its fame to a psychic investigator named Harry Price. Jenny Randles and Peter Hough write of Price, "That he courted the media cannot be denied, and evidence that he exaggerated and sometimes cheated to hype up the hauntings at Borley seems fairly substantial."[9]

In at least some instances, this is how ghostly legends are born. There may have been some mysterious goings-on at Borley Rectory, but chances are they were magnified and exaggerated with each successive telling, and then twisted even more by an over-zealous "investigator." This seems to happen repeatedly with "ghost stories" and other tales of the supernatural.

This may even be the case with the story of Larry and Susan that we discussed earlier.

Have you ever had the experience of hearing someone describe an event that the two of you attended together and found yourself wondering how they could be so far off target? It's a natural tendency for people to confuse and exaggerate events. That's just human nature. For that reason it's entirely possible the whole story is nothing more than a series of coincidences, spurred along by an overactive imagination. Perhaps it's true that Larry bought a house and found out later that the previous owner had committed suicide in the basement. Maybe his sons had an imaginary friend they called "the old man," who really was nothing more than a figment of their imaginations. Perhaps events like these began to come together in Larry's mind and made the story much bigger than it really was.

On the other hand, it's also possible that Larry's home may be "haunted" by some mysterious entity of unknown origin. After all, there are some ghost experiences that seem to defy natural explanation. Poltergeists, for instance.

Poltergeists

Poltergeists appear to be noisy, destructive, and malicious. They're called the "practical jokers" of the supernatural world, allegedly pulling pranks that are frightening and expensive.

Poltergeists have been reported to throw things around, break dishes, and move furniture, and there have been several, well-documented cases of such activity.

One of the most famous poltergeist disturbances of the past few decades took place in Bristol, Connecticut, over a two-week period. The victims were a couple named John and Susan Sanford and their two sons. During that time dishes supposedly flew out of cupboards and were smashed on the floor, pictures fell from walls throughout the house, and furniture rearranged itself. The family also reported hearing growling noises and seeing red eyes peering in at them through the living room window.

A photographer named Paul Eno who went to investigate the phenomena said that when he was in the house, he felt something like a strong electrical current that made his hair stand on end. When his film was developed, one of the photographs allegedly showed a bearded face looking into the house through a window.[10]

Regardless of whomever or whatever was responsible for the strange activity in the house, it didn't last long. It stopped just as suddenly as it began—a common occurrence with poltergeists.

Another Name

Again, no one knows for sure what poltergeists are. Some feel they are spirits that feed off fear and hate. However, the Bible has another name for spirits of this type. They're called—you guessed it—*demons.*

And, as we covered in chapter 3, no demon is a match for the power and authority of Jesus Christ.

One woman told me about a terrifying experience she had when she was in her early 20s. She wasn't a Christian at the time, although she knew about Jesus Christ and the Bible's claims that he died for the sins of all mankind. She said she woke up in the middle of the night feeling extremely cold and terrified. Immediately she knew that something evil was in her bedroom. Her eyes flew open, and she saw a gargoyle-like creature standing at the foot of her bed. It was like nothing she had ever seen before, and she will never forget the utter hatred that shone in the creature's vicious, terrifying eyes.

"Jesus!" she cried. "Help me!"

Immediately the creature vanished. Her bedroom was perceptibly warmer, and she no longer felt afraid. She remains convinced that this was *not* a dream or a hallucination. Something evil had invaded her room, but it had disappeared the instant she called upon the name of Jesus.

Shortly after her ghostly encounter, this woman began to read the Bible and pray on a regular basis. It wasn't long before she surrendered her life to Christ, and today she is a missionary, serving him in France.

Another woman tells of being awakened in the middle of the night by a force pressing down on her body. She couldn't see anything, but she could feel ghostly hands pushing down on her.

When she tried to struggle against her attacker, she found she couldn't move, nor could she open her mouth to scream. She seemed paralyzed, completely powerless against her ghostly assailant.

She was, however, able to pray a silent prayer: "Please … God … in the name of Jesus … help me!"

At that moment the attack stopped. The pressure lifted, and she leaped out of bed, flipped on the light, and saw that the room was empty.

She spent the rest of the night in her living room, with all the lights on, but her attacker did not return.

Ghosts and the Bible

Occasionally someone will point to what they say are references to ghosts in the Bible. There are two specific passages they cite as proof that ghosts are the souls of the departed.

The first is chapter 17 of Matthew, which tells us that when Jesus was transfigured, and Moses and Elijah (both had been dead for hundreds of years) appeared and talked with him. But, as we mentioned before, this passage isn't about proving the existence of ghosts. It's about Jesus preparing for the cross and the proof that he is greater than anyone who lived before him—even Moses and Elijah.

The second Scripture cited is chapter 28 of 1 Samuel. This passage tells of King Saul's visit to the medium at Endor, who summoned for him the spirit of the prophet Samuel. Obviously, according to Deuteronomy 18:10–12, Saul was going *way* against God's law by visiting the medium. But in this instance, it seems that God allowed the deceased prophet to appear and give a very important message to the king. That message was, "You have sinned, and God is going to take the kingdom away from you."

Actually, neither one of these passages has anything to do with ghosts or haunted houses. In both instances the appearance of spirits of the dead was *brought about by a sovereign act of God.* You see, God can do whatever he wants to do, however he chooses to do it.

All human souls, both the living and the dead, are under his control.

The Bottom Line

Although what we believe about ghosts is important, it's not nearly as important as what we believe about the messages that come through them. Remember what I've said before: Any creature, whether physical or spiritual in nature, that denies the divinity of Jesus Christ—or that says things in direct contradiction to God's Word—can't be trusted.

When it comes to ghosts—or any other supernatural entity—it's vital that we test the spirits, according to 1 John 4, and remember the apostle Paul's words from the first chapter of Galatians:

> But even if we or an angel from heaven should preach a gospel other than the one we preached to you, let them be under God's curse! As we have already said, so now I say again: If anybody is preaching to you a gospel other than what you accepted, let them be under God's curse!
>
> Galatians 1:8–9

In the 1960s James A. Pike, a bishop in the Episcopal Church, became an outspoken advocate of "communicating with spirits" and other occult practices. The bishop became a champion of the occult largely through what he believed to be encounters with the ghost of his son, who had died of a drug overdose.

The "spirit" of Bishop Pike's son reportedly told him, with regret in his voice, that he wished he could tell his father that Jesus was Lord and victorious over all, but that it just wasn't true. He also told the bishop that even "on the other side," there were pockets of "believers" who still considered Christ to be their Savior and who waited patiently for his second coming. But, of course, they were fools who were humored and pitied by all the truly enlightened ones.

On his son's say-so, Bishop Pike turned away from his faith in Christ. Sadly, through his numerous books, articles, and TV appearances, he undoubtedly moved many others away from faith in the Lord as well.

And yet the Bible is clear on this. If *anyone*—human, angel, space alien, or ghost—tells us we can be saved some other way than through faith in Christ, he's a liar and a tool of Satan, not to be trusted.

I've said before that I don't know what ghosts are. That's true. But I do *not* believe for a minute they're the spirits of dead people.

Once again, take a look at what the Bible says:

> Just as people are destined to die once, and after that to face judgment, so Christ was sacrificed once to take away the sins of many; and he will appear a second time, not to bear sin, but to bring salvation to those who are waiting for him.
>
> Hebrews 9:27–28

That couldn't be any clearer. After a man dies he is judged, and then he is sent to the appropriate place of reward or punishment.

There's no stopping by the house of an old friend to put in some guest appearances or play a few games on a Ouija board. Nor will there be any visits to the home of an old enemy to rattle a few chains and give some chills.

Do you remember Jesus' parable about the rich man and Lazarus? After the rich man died and was judged, he was sent to a place of torment. He begged Abraham to come to him and cool his tongue with a few drops of water, but Abraham couldn't do it.

Abraham told him:

> Son, remember that in your lifetime you received your good things, while Lazarus received bad things, but now he is comforted here and you are in agony. And besides all this, between us and you a great chasm has been set in place, so that those who want to go from here to you cannot, nor can anyone cross over from there to us.
>
> Luke 16:25–26

There is a great "chasm" that exists between heaven and hell and between this life and the next. For that reason alone I won't listen to any creature that says it has come from "the life beyond" to enlighten me.

I may not know what ghosts are, but I do know enough not to listen to what they say.

There's no doubt that the subject of ghosts and haunted houses is a fascinating one. But it can also be dangerous. An interest in ghosts can open a door into the world of the occult which is better left closed. A ghost who seems as gentle as Casper may, in reality, be a demon who is anxious to mislead us —to convince us that it doesn't really matter what we believe.

And as Jesus Christ said time and time again, it does matter. It's the difference between an eternity in heaven or in hell.

1. Statistics taken from "Poll: Majority believe in ghosts". Sean Alfano. February 11, 2009. http://www.cbsnews.com/2100-500160_162-994766.html
2. Statistics taken from "Boo! One in three people believes in ghosts" Associated Press. October 25, 2007. http://www.msnbc.msn.com/id/21477704/ns/health-behavior/t/boo-one-three-people-believes-ghosts
3. Klimo, 37.
4. Randles and Hough, 112.
5. Randles and Hough, 113.
6. Randles and Hough, 113.
7. Randles and Hough, 114-115.
8. Randles and Hough, 146.
9. Randles and Hough, 143.
10. Randles and Hough, 129–130.

8

Near-Death Experiences

Joyce Evans is alive and living in England. But no one will ever be able to convince her that she didn't "die" in 1972, when complications arose during the birth of her son, David.[1]

David was delivered through cesarean section when just about everything that could go wrong did. Mrs. Evans' doctor told her later that he considered her survival a miracle.

What Joyce remembers is that all of a sudden, she found herself traveling rapidly through a dark tunnel, approaching a bright light at the other end.

"I knew very clearly that I was dying. There was beautiful music playing; the air was filled with it. The light at the end of the tunnel was very bright," Joyce says. "I can remember thinking, *It's the end of the line for you*, yet I felt absolutely no fear."

When she reached the end of the tunnel, Joyce was overjoyed to see her father waiting there, smiling at her, looking exactly the way she remembered him from her childhood. She recognized him immediately, even though he had been dead for fourteen years.

"I was so pleased to see him and be with him, and there was an overwhelming feeling of peace and tranquility," Joyce remembers. But just before she reached his side, he put his hand up to stop her.

"It's not your time," he said. "Go back! Go back! You have a baby who needs you."

Joyce doesn't remember anything further until she found herself regaining consciousness in her hospital room. She was very ill and had a long period of recuperation facing her. Still, she was happy to be alive. She didn't want to leave her husband or children.

"I felt I had been given a second chance," she says. "But at the same time, I also know that I've seen what death is like, and there's nothing to be afraid of. I saw how well and happy my father looked, and that was very reassuring. But most of all, I remember the lovely feeling I had all the time I was in the tunnel."

An Experience Shared by Many

Millions of people around the world say they've had experiences similar to the one Joyce Evans describes. Today we call them near-death experiences or NDEs. A Gallup Poll revealed that an estimated eight million Americans have had these experiences, and many tell stories quite similar to the one Joyce Evans told.[2]

They, too, remember traveling through a dark tunnel, racing toward a bright light at the other end. They often tell of seeing dead relatives waiting for them in the light. Sometimes they see Jesus or a benevolent being "of light" whom they believe to be Jesus. Then they hear a voice, or someone comes to them and tells them they have to go back. And the next thing they know, they're back in the operating room, or at the site of the car crash, or wherever they were when they "died."

Most also say they were very disappointed when they were told they couldn't stay. Unlike Joyce, they didn't want to come back. They also report that the experience has changed them forever. They no longer fear death. And finally, many say they understand how important it is to be loving and kind.

One man, interviewed on his near-death experience, said:

> If my wife was listening I would have to tell you that the most important thing that ever happened to me was meeting and marrying her. But the truth is my NDE is the most important event in my life. It changed me more than any other thing. It shaped me. It changed my personality—and even though my wife has been trying for years to do that, she's never succeeded. Having an NDE is the most profound thing anyone could go through, apart from death itself.[3]

An Old Story Becomes New

Even though near-death experiences have been around for centuries, it was only around forty years ago that they became really big news. That's when Raymond A. Moody, Jr. published a book titled *Life After Life.* Dr. Moody decided to write his book when several people who had been resuscitated after "dying" told him about amazing experiences they'd had.

Life After Life sold millions of copies all over the world and began an intense debate on the nature and believability of such accounts. His book was hailed as a breakthrough because it was the first time anyone from the scientific community seemed to take the phenomena of near-death experiences seriously. Dr. Moody had removed near-death experiences from the realm of myth, folklore, and superstition and made them respectable.

As for Dr. Moody, he was convinced something very real had happened to these people who had "died" and then come back to life. He didn't try to explain it away or chalk the whole thing up to imagination or hallucination. And he came very close to insisting these experiences were proof of life after death.

In *Life After Life* Dr. Moody lists several common characteristics of the typical near-death experience. These include:

- An awareness of being dead.
- A feeling of peace and freedom from pain.
- A journey through a tunnel.
- Emergence from the tunnel into a world of light, peace, and tranquility.
- An encounter with a "being of light," who radiates love and understanding.
- A review of the life the person has lived.
- A rapid return to the body.[4]

What Should We Think about Near-Death Experiences?

In the stories Dr. Moody collected, almost all had one other common element: They were nearly all positive—barely one frightening moment in the whole bunch.

Certainly it would be wonderful to think we have nothing to fear from death. Wouldn't it be great to believe we were all going to wind up in a happy place, where the sun shines all the time and everything is beautiful? But on the other hand, would that be fair? Could it really be true that it doesn't matter what we believe or what we do during this life?

The fact is, not every near-death experience is peaceful and serene. Some of them are downright terrifying.

Researcher Dr. Michael Grosso, who has interviewed dozens of people who have had near-death experiences, tells about a man who tried to kill himself with an overdose of drugs and suffered a massive heart attack as a result.[5] Friends found him and quickly called paramedics. But by the time they arrived, his heart had stopped; he wasn't breathing; and his body had already turned blue.

According to his account, his soul was on a journey to a place he never wants to see again. There was no tunnel, no bright light, and no comforting presence. Instead the man found himself descending into an inferno, where horrible-looking creatures grabbed and scratched at him with their claws. He later recalled he had a difficult time breathing and felt claustrophobic.

Fortunately for him, paramedics were able to get his heart beating again, and he suddenly found himself back in his body. He said he had made significant changes in his lifestyle because he didn't want to go back to that horrible place.

They Don't Remember a Thing

Cardiologist Maurice Rawlings, in his book *Beyond Death's Door*, writes:

> Before gathering material for this book, I personally regarded most after-death experiences as fantasy or conjecture or imagination. Most of the cases I had heard or read about sounded as if they represented euphoric trips of an anoxic mind. Then one evening in 1977 I was resuscitating a terrified patient who told me he was actually in hell. He begged me to get him out of hell and not let him die. When I fully realized how genuinely and extremely frightened he was, I too became frightened. Subsequent cases with terrifying experiences have burdened me with a sense of urgency to write this book. Now I feel assured that there is life after death, and not all of it is good.[6]

Dr. Rawlings describes the patient discussed above as having "a grotesque grimace expressing sheer horror. His pupils were dilating and he was perspiring and trembling—he looked as if his hair was 'on end.'"[7]

The doctor worked feverishly to save the man's life—and succeeded. As a cardiologist he's accustomed to life-or-death situations. But he couldn't get this frightening experience out of his mind. That's why, a few days later, when the patient was stabilized, the doctor asked him why he had been so frightened. Had he seen flames or monsters? Perhaps even the devil himself?

But surprisingly enough the man didn't know what his doctor was talking about. He didn't remember a thing.

Dr. Rawlings writes, "Apparently, the experiences were so frightening, so horrible, so painful that his conscious mind could not cope with them; and they were subsequently repressed far into his subconscious."[8]

Dr. Rawlings now believes, from his experience with this patient and others like him, that "when patient interviews are delayed in any way, this may allow enough time for the good experiences to be mentally retained and reported by the patient and the bad experiences to be rejected or obliterated from recall."[9]

He has also come to believe terrifying near-death experiences may be just as common as the positive ones, and he reports that some of the patients he has brought back from the edge of death actually do remember a few details of their negative experiences. They recall entering a dark, dim world, where grotesque people lurk in the shadows or stand along the shore of a lake of fire. He says, "The horrors defy description and are difficult to recall."[10]

For some people the horror has been the realization they were heading away from God instead of toward him. *Beyond Death's Door* tells the story of a woman who was struck by lightning while on a camping trip. She says:

> In the moment that I was hit, I knew exactly what had happened to me. My mind was crystal clear. I had never been so totally alive as in the act of dying. At this point in the act of dying, I had what I call the answer to a question I had never verbalized to anyone

> or even faced: Is there really a God? I can't describe it, but the totality and the reality of the living God exploded within my being and He filled every atom of my body with his glory. In the next moment, to my horror, I found that I wasn't going toward God. I was going away from Him. It was like seeing what might have been, but going away from it.[11]

In her panic this woman says she cried out to God, telling him she would live for him from now on if he would spare her life. He did. She found herself back in her body and within three months, had completely recovered.

Nobody Thinks They'll Go to Hell

Jean Ritchie, in her book *Death's Door*, cites a study in which modern accounts of near-death experiences were compared with those recorded in medieval times. Many elements were the same: the feeling of being out of the body, traveling through a tunnel, undergoing a review of one's life. But that study found one major difference … in medieval times, negative experiences were far more frequent. People spoke more often of seeing demons, devils, and hell.

Why the difference between then and now?

One theory is that back then, people believed in hell. Now, for the most part, they don't. A few hundred years ago, people who lived sinful lives knew full well they were going to wind up in hell when they died. They were prepared for it and, in fact, expected it. Today most people seem to have the attitude that a loving God would never send anyone to hell. We think, *It doesn't really matter what I do. God will forgive me.* We expect the pearly gates of heaven to swing open for us the moment we die.

It could be that people don't see hell simply because they don't believe in it. This could mean either of two things:

1. A near-death experience is really nothing more than a

hallucination that has no real connection to what happens after we die.

2. People who are given a glimpse of hell are so shocked and stunned by the sight of something they never believed in—nor thought would ever happen to them—that their minds simply can't retain it.

What the Bible Says about Death

If we believe the Bible, we must also believe in the existence of hell. Jesus taught that hell exists. He said that on the day of judgment, the unrighteous "will go away to eternal punishment, but the righteous to eternal life" (Matthew 25:46).

He also said, "If your hand causes you to stumble, cut it off. It is better for you to enter life maimed than with two hands to go into hell, where the fire never goes out" (Mark 9:43).

The book of Revelation tells us that when the dead are judged, anyone whose name isn't written in the book of life will be thrown into the lake of fire (Revelation 20:15).

The Bible also seems to teach that some will be able to escape hell by the narrowest of margins, as happened to the man Dr. Rawlings revived. The apostle Paul says that on the day of judgment, each man's "work" will be tested by fire: "If what he has built survives, he will receive his reward. If it is burned up, he will suffer loss; he himself will be saved, but only as one escaping through the flames" (1 Corinthians 3:14–15).

As we can see, the Bible tells us that hell is a very real place. And so is heaven.

Jesus told his disciples:

> Do not let your hearts be troubled. You believe in God; believe also in me. In my Father's house are many rooms; if that were not so, would have told that I am going there to prepare a place for you?

> And if I go and prepare a place for you, I will come back and take you with me that you also may be where I am.
>
> (John 14:1–3)

Jesus also said that on the day of judgment, the righteous will be told, "'Come, you who are blessed by my Father; take your inheritance, the kingdom prepared for you since the creation of the world" (Matthew 25:34).

The Bible not only tells us that heaven exists, but it also gives clear-cut directions for getting there. We've probably heard this a million times, but it makes it no less true: "For God so loved the world that he gave his one and only Son, that whoever believes in him shall not perish but have eternal life" (John 3:16).

When Jesus told his disciples they would follow him to heaven, Thomas objected, "'Lord, we don't know where you are going, so how can we know the way?'

"Jesus answered, 'I am the way and the truth and the life. No one comes to the Father except through me'" (John 14:4–6).

Even though the Bible says that those who have accepted Christ will go to heaven—and those who haven't accepted him will not—it doesn't tell us exactly when this will happen, nor does it say precisely what occurs the moment we die. What it does tell us is that "people are destined to die once, and after that to face judgment" (Hebrews 9:27).

Some believe that when we die, we go to a holding area, a place of sorting, to await that judgment. If this is true, it's likely that those who have had near-death experiences have only experienced the holding area and haven't truly glimpsed their final destination.

In *Beyond Death's Door,* Maurice Rawlings writes:

> It is interesting that all of my patients who report a continuance from one life to another, whether it was good or bad, usually met previous loved ones in a type of sorting place that often

had a barrier preventing entrance into a more permanent type of existence.[12]

Of course no one wants to hear bad news. It would be easy for us to look at all the positive stories and say, "Life after death is just great for everybody!" But we can't let selected experiences take precedence over what the Bible says. God's Word is the final authority in everything—especially matters of life after death.

A Word About Suicide ... DON'T!

Incidentally, Dr. Rawlings says there's one area in which near-death experiences have been almost universally negative, and that is in cases involving attempted suicide. He tells of a 14-year-old girl who tried to kill herself by gulping down an entire bottle full of aspirin. As doctors fought to save her life, she cried out, "Mama, help me! They're trying to hurt me!" She also said that those "demons in hell" had hold of her and wouldn't let her go. Later, after she had completely recovered, she remembered nothing of the incident.[13]

In *Life After Life*, Dr. Moody writes:

> A man who was despondent about the death of his wife shot himself, "died" as a result and was resuscitated. He states: "I didn't go where [my wife] was. I went to an awful place.... I immediately saw the mistake I had made.... I thought, 'I wish I hadn't done it.'"[14]

Another woman who took an overdose of drugs reported:

> I remember going down this black hole, round and round. Then I saw a glowing, red-hot spot getting bigger and bigger until I was able to stand up. It was all red and hot and on fire. The earth was like slimy mud that sank over my feet and it was hard to move. The heat was awful and made it hard to breathe. I cried, "Oh, Lord, give me another chance." I prayed and prayed. How I got back, I'll never know.[15]

Do I mean to suggest that all suicide victims go to hell?

Of course not.

God alone is the judge of that. But these experiences seem to back up the truth that suicide is always the worst way out of any problem.

What Science Says

Before we leave the subject of near-death experiences, I think it's important to note that many experts believe there's a scientific basis for them that has nothing to do with life after death. Instead, they feel such experiences occur during the dying process, when the brain is shutting down. They say the sensation of flying through a tunnel could be the result of the collapse of the visual field in the occipital lobe. Some scientists also believe the light that seems to shine at the end of the tunnel may be produced by a lack of oxygen.

Dr. Susan Blackmore of the Brain and Perception Laboratory at Bristol University in England points out that the visual cortex of the brain is one of the last areas to die and says:

> The vital cells that normally regulate the activity in the visual sector of the brain—the visual cortex—are seriously inhibited by the increasing lack of sensory information. This destabilizes the normal visual controls, producing stripes of irregular activity. As this information travels between the retina of the eye and the brain, the stripes are interpreted as being concentric rings, tunnels or undulating spirals, light in the center and darker at the edges.... The mind latches on to these tunnel images and accepts them as a new actuality.[16]

The Bottom Line

There's no way to know for sure, this side of heaven, exactly what near-death experiences are. The only thing we *can* know for certain is that Christians have absolutely no reason to fear death. We can have confidence in the words of Jesus, who said, "I am going there to prepare a place for you" (John 14:2).

As we wrap up this chapter, I think of the death of Dwight L. Moody, one of the most famous evangelists America has ever produced. As he lay dying, Moody shouted out, "Earth recedes! Heaven opens before me!" And then, turning to his son, "This is no dream, Will. It is beautiful! If this is death, it is sweet. God is calling me and I must go! Don't call me back!"[17]

Truly, for Christians, "'Death has been swallowed up in victory'" (1 Corinthians 15:54).

---

1. Jean Ritchie, *Death's Door* (New York: Bantam Doubleday Dell Publishing Group, Inc., 1994) 75–76.
2. Randles and Hough, 226.
3. Ritchie, 20.
4. Raymond A. Moody, Jr., M.D., *Life After Life* (Harrisburg, PA: Stackpole Books, 1976).
5. Randles and Hough, 223.
6. Maurice Rawlings, M.D., *Beyond Death's Door* (New York: Bantam Books, 1978) xii-xiii.
7. Rawlings, 3.
8. Rawlings, 5.
9. Rawlings, 6.
10. Rawlings, 45.
11. Rawlings, 64.
12. Rawlings, 35.
13. Rawlings, 94–95.
14. Moody, 143.
15. Rawlings, 96.
16. Phillips, 231
17. Rawlings, 53–54.

9

Reincarnation

In India and other Asian countries where Hinduism and Buddhism are prominent, reincarnation has long been accepted as fact. But for America it got a real boost in the early 1950s with Bridey Murphy.

It was 1952, to be exact, when a man named Morey Bernstein hypnotized a young woman named Virginia Tighe.

While she was under hypnosis, Bernstein told his patient to go back to the time she was a little girl. In response she began to talk and act like a five-year-old. When he told her that she was now an infant, she started gurgling and cooing like one.

That's when Bernstein tried something daring. He told the woman that he wanted her to keep going back—to the time before she was born. I don't know what Bernstein expected, but he says he got the shock of his life when his patient suddenly began speaking in a strong Irish brogue. She told him her name was Bridey Murphy and that she was living in a small village in

Ireland—in the 1700s. She described the house and village in which she lived and told minute details about her life.

There were several more sessions during which Bernstein took Ms. Tighe back to eighteenth-century Ireland. Every time, the young woman gave her name as Bridey Murphy. She sang Irish songs and told Irish stories, all in the most convincing Irish accent.

Bernstein wrote about the experience in a best-selling book titled *The Search for Bridey Murphy*, and it started a furor. Many people were convinced that Bernstein's story was proof of reincarnation. The study of "past lives" became a hot topic—and big business. Everywhere, hypnotists were finding that what Bernstein said was true. When their clients were taken back, through hypnotism, to the time before they were born, they invariably told clear details of what seemed to be previous lives.

Who Was Bridey Murphy?

So what about Bridey Murphy? Did she ever really exist? Several newspapers sent reporters to Ireland to investigate, but none of them were able to find the slightest bit of evidence. If she ever really lived there, she left nothing at all to mark her existence—not even a tombstone.

That lack of concrete proof didn't bother those who wanted to believe in reincarnation. Bridey Murphy had become something of a "poster child" for reincarnation, and they weren't about to let her go. They pointed out that her story had the ring of authenticity. Where, they asked, could she have learned such exacting details about rural life in 1700s Ireland unless she had lived there?

Apparently they never considered the possibilities: books, movies, plays, school, or magazines. Maybe even ... a neighbor.

According to the *Chicago American* newspaper, the latter

is exactly where the "myth" of Bridey Murphy came from—a neighbor. While all of their competitors were in Ireland looking for Ms. Murphy, a reporter for the *American* apparently found her right at home ... in Chicago. He discovered a woman named Bridie Murphy Corkell lived in the house across the street from where Virginia Tighe grew up. What Virginia remembered under hypnosis was apparently not from a former life, but rather bits and pieces of information she had learned while she was a little girl.

Any Strange Dreams Lately?

What we might conclude from this is that Virginia Tighe's past-life memory was really the product of what psychologists call *cryptomnesia*. Cryptomnesia refers to the human brain's ability to store every piece of information it encounters, no matter how random or trivial that information might be. Sometimes this information is stored deep down in the subconscious, making it possible for us to know things we don't even know we know. Occasionally bits and pieces of this information may get scrambled together into a confusing mess.

Have you ever had a really strange dream? You woke up and thought, *Wow! Where did that one come from?* But after you thought about it for a while, you could see all sorts of things that had happened to you during the day had been put together into the craziest dream since Pharaoh's.

I've had that experience many times, and I've also noticed some of the information and events that made their way into my dream were majorly trivial. I didn't realize they had even made a dent in my subconscious when I first experienced them. Obviously the impact was greater than I suspected, or I wouldn't have wound up dreaming about them.

Not too long ago I dreamed I was a doctor, working on a very primitive Native American reservation somewhere in Arizona or New Mexico. The dream was quite vivid and real. For a few seconds after I woke up, I thought I really was a doctor and was even a bit worried about some of the patients I had been treating. Later on, when I looked back on the dream, I could see that it was assembled from fragments of information my mind was trying to process—information from a book, a fundraising letter I read, a few minutes of a television show, and probably quite a few other places.

Now suppose I had been hypnotized when all of this information was fresh on my mind and taken back to the time before I was born as Bill Myers? I might have remembered my days in the Old West, perhaps as a Native American or a settler living among the Native Americans.

This is apparently what happened to another woman, who, under hypnosis, impressed the experts with stories about her life as Livonia, a Roman citizen of the late third century. Her story was so impressive that it was even featured in a book and television show.

But a researcher named Melvin Harris started combing through libraries, looking for information on ancient Rome that might have found its way into the woman's memories. He found it in two historical novels written by Louis de Wohl years before the past-life regression. De Wohl's novels not only contained facts regarding daily life in Rome during the third century but also included many of the characters and events that had filled the woman's "past-life memory."[1]

Had she been intentionally trying to deceive?

I doubt it.

Remember, she was under hypnosis. But her hypnotist had asked her to do something that was impossible, which was to go back in time before she was born. When that happened, her mind apparently latched onto information she had read years before and then "forgotten."

What Does the Bible Teach?

There's no evidence to support a belief in reincarnation. But some people are going to believe in it no matter what. They even point to the third chapter of John as proof that Jesus taught it. The passage in question involves Jesus' encounter with Nicodemus, a member of the Jewish ruling council:

> Jesus declared, "I tell you the truth, no one can see the kingdom of God unless they are born again."
>
> "How can someone be born when they are old?" Nicodemus asked. "Surely he cannot enter a second time into his mother's womb to be born!"
>
> Jesus answered, "Very truly I tell you, no one can enter the kingdom of God unless they are born of water and the Spirit. Flesh gives birth to flesh, but the Spirit gives birth to spirit. You should not be surprised at my saying, 'You must be born again.' The wind blows wherever it pleases. You hear its sound, but you cannot tell where it comes from or where it is going. So it is with everyone born of the Spirit."
>
> John 3:3–8

There is *not one serious Bible scholar* who believes Jesus is talking about anything other than the rebirth process that takes place in our spirit when we put our trust in Christ. This verse definitely does not refer to reincarnation. In fact ...

Reincarnation Opposes Jesus Christ

- Jesus says that anyone who accepts what he did for them on the cross and follows him is immediately clean of all their wrongs and guilt. Reincarnation teaches the sins committed in past lifetimes must be worked off by that person in the next, until he finally reaches a state of holiness and purity.
- Jesus says that once we die, those who accept the work he did for them on the cross and follow him will go to heaven to live forever with God. Those who don't will live forever apart from God. Reincarnation says we'll all live again and again here on earth until we get everything right.
- The Bible teaches that "people are destined to die *once*, and after that to face judgment" (Hebrews 9:27, emphasis mine). According to reincarnation, we die again and again. There is really no judgment, only karma, which will be dealt with in our next life.

In short, reincarnation leaves no room for Christ's death on the cross. If reincarnation were true, it would mean Christ's death was useless. We'd have no need for anyone to save us if we can reach perfection on our own over dozens or hundreds of lifetimes.

Nowhere does the Bible even hint that reincarnation might be true. Instead, it stresses again and again that every human being is a unique individual created in the image of God himself.

And yet, more and more Americans seem to be accepting this imported Eastern belief as fact, including many Christians.

A 1984 Gallup Poll showed that fewer than forty million Americans believed in reincarnation. By 1991 the number of American believers had reached fifty million. That's more than ten million new adherents in just seven years. And according to a Pew Forum report, 24 percent of Americans (and 22 percent of Christians) believe in reincarnation today—that's about one out of four Americans.[2]

A friend of mine, a guy who says he believes in Christ and attends church every Sunday, recently told me about a deceased relative who had a very sad life. He said he hoped she would have a happier life "the next time around."

When I challenged him on this, he bristled and said that he didn't see anything wrong with reincarnation—after all, "God never said it isn't true." My response was that Christ may not have addressed reincarnation per se, but there's simply no way to align his teachings, or the rest of the Bible's teachings, with reincarnation.

Still, my friend's attitude isn't uncommon. Several recent books attempt to make belief in reincarnation palatable to Christians. The theme of these books is always the same: the early church fathers accepted reincarnation as a fact, but over the centuries this truth became perverted, twisted, and eventually lost.

That's simply not true.

As we've already seen, there's absolutely no way to hold to a belief in reincarnation and to Christ's sacrificial death on the cross. But, thanks in large part to books, the media, and celebrities, belief in reincarnation and past-lives regression continues growing in popularity.

The Problem with Karma

But forget the popular culture—what does the Bible say?

It teaches that every individual is responsible for his own actions in this life. He isn't going to suffer in this life because of something he did in a previous existence, as reincarnation teaches. That common Eastern belief is known as "karma," and it causes incredible suffering throughout the world.

Take the Hindu country of Nepal. When a child is born into a poor family or with a disability or sickness, his neighbors think it's due to some sin he committed in a previous life. No one will offer a helping hand. Why should they? If a child is suffering because of bad karma, it's because his soul is being purified, and it would be wrong to try to help him.

When I visited Nepal, I was shocked to see dozens of desperately poor children living on the streets by themselves. When I asked about these kids, I was told they were orphans who had been expelled from their village.

"But why?" I demanded.

The explanation was infuriating.

When a child is orphaned, it's considered to be his fault from a past life. Instead of helping him, his neighbors throw him out of their village and forbid him to come back. They think they're being kind. They're hoping the child will go off somewhere and quietly starve to death. Then, once his short, unhappy life is over—and he will have paid for his bad karma—he can be reborn into a better life. These starving children eat handfuls of dirt in an attempt to stop the hunger pains that tear at their stomachs. It's an outrageous tragedy, and it's due to the belief in reincarnation.

I know a Christian missionary in Nepal who goes by the name of Simon Peter. Now, being a missionary in a country like Nepal is taking your life into your hands. Until a few years ago, it was against the law to even talk about Jesus to anyone outside of your immediate family. If you were caught speaking to a non-relative about Christ, you could spend a year in prison. If you helped someone become a Christian or baptized them, you could be thrown into prison for up to six years.

So what did Simon Peter do? He went out and adopted dozens of orphans—children whose villages were just waiting for them to die. Once they were officially his sons and daughters, he was legally free to teach these children about Christ. To date, this incredible man has legally adopted eighty of these little ones nobody wanted.

Many are grown now, and most, if not all, are on fire for God. Some have graduated from Bible colleges. Others have started churches. Needless to say, they take what Jesus did for them on the cross very seriously, knowing firsthand how awful life would be if they had to suffer for their own sins through the brutality of reincarnation.

Trust Hypnotism?

Before we leave the subject of reincarnation, let's go back for just a moment to revisit the whole idea of exploring past lives through hypnotism.

What happens when we allow ourselves to be put into a hypnotic trance? Basically, we surrender control of our minds to another person. Some experts believe hypnotism is dangerous for precisely this reason. Especially as Scripture tells us to surrender ourselves to no one but God.

Researcher Robert A. Morey states, "A hypnotic trance is the exact mental state which mediums and witches have been self-inducing for centuries in order to open themselves up to spirit or demonic control. Hypnotic regression to a 'past life' can easily be an occult experience."

He continues with another sober observation:

> Here lies the ultimate explanation for those "unexplainable" recall cases. In every situation where a person recalled a "past life," and this life was researched and proven factual in even intimate

> details, and not fraudulent, the person was involved in occult practices. Supernatural knowledge was gained by contact with satanic beings.[3]

Don't get me wrong. I'm not saying that all hypnotism is wrong. For me, the jury is still out on this. However, I *am* saying it's a dangerous area and anything that happens to a person who is under hypnosis should be viewed with extreme skepticism.

I've never been hypnotized, nor do I intend to be, so I'll never know what it's like. But an acquaintance who went under hypnosis because she was writing a magazine article on the subject said it was an experience she'll never forget.

The hypnotist told her she was sitting beside a clear stream in a mountain setting. She remembered that when he said this, she could see the spot clearly and described it as one of the most beautiful places she had ever been. Then he told her to dangle her toes in the water.

"I could actually feel it," she told me. "It was cold and wet … It was real!"

But it wasn't real at all. That's the danger with hypnotism. Besides flirting with the occult, it also blurs the lines between reality and fantasy. It's capable of distorting the truth and making us believe a lie. It can make us think we're beside a beautiful mountain stream, when we're really sitting in a sterile office building in downtown Los Angeles. And it can make us believe that we've lived before—in ancient Ireland or perhaps Rome.

To Sum Up

Half of the world's population believes in reincarnation. But that doesn't make it any less a lie. We've seen that a belief in reincarnation is dangerous for several reasons:

1. It lets people off the hook for their choices. According to reincarnation, if we mess up in this life, we can always do better next time around.
2. It encourages us to ignore people's needs. According to karma, if someone is hurting, they deserve it because of something they did in a past life. Better to let them suffer, die, and move on to the next life.
3. It denies the importance of Jesus dying on the cross for our sins. It completely opposes what he says about him being the only way to get cleaned up and be with God.

Remember what the Bible says? "People are destined to die once, and after that to face judgment" (Hebrews 9:27).

Not *many* deaths, but *one* death. Not *many* judgments, but *one* judgment.

And there's only one way to ensure we will pass through this judgment without harm. Back to those famous words of Jesus:

> For God so loved the world that he gave his one and only Son, that whoever believes in him shall not perish but have eternal life. For God did not send his Son into the world to condemn the world, but to save the world through him.
>
> John 3:16–17

---

1. Randles and Hough, 195–197.

2. Pew Forum statistics taken from "Many Americans Mix Multiple Faiths: Eastern, New Age Beliefs Widespread," Pew Forum on Religious and Spiritual Life, December 9, 2009. http://pewforum.org/Other-Beliefs-and-Practices/Many-Americans-Mix-Multiple-Faiths.aspx

3. Robert A. Morey, *Reincarnation and Christianity* (Minneapolis: Bethany House Publishers, 1980) 24–25.

10

Wicca and Witchcraft

Although there are some differences between Wicca and witchcraft, in the interest of space, we'll be lumping them together and not delving into the finer distinctions. Regardless, if there are any counterfeits that make my blood boil, it's witchcraft — not because it's more dangerous than the others, but because it preys mostly on girls who are trying to find their way in life. It's tough enough to be a teenage girl in our culture with all the pressures of:

- having a certain appearance
- dressing a certain way
- getting the right grades
- getting the attention of boys
- being popular enough
- belonging to the right cliques
- dealing with parents

- having the perfect body
- having the perfect hair
- having the perfect everything!

And that's just what I see as an outside observer. I can't imagine what it's like to actually live it.

Imagine what it would be like to have someone suddenly offer love, acceptance, no rules, an appreciation of nature, and most importantly *a way to have total power over your life.*

Who *wouldn't* be attracted to this?

Both witchcraft and Wicca make these very offers, but like every other occult practice, in reality they're just baited hooks. There are lots of promises on the outside, and they often come with a certain satisfaction at the beginning, but *only* at the beginning—only until the hooks are swallowed and the destroyer starts to slowly reel in the person.

Oh, our enemy may not kill physically, but over the months, sometimes years, girls who try to find power in their lives through witchcraft, are frequently left behind their peers both socially and emotionally. While others mature and learn how to deal with life's difficulties on a real basis, those caught up in Wicca's lies about a shortcut to power often wind up having to play catch-up in dealing and coping with the realities of life.

That's why I believe God hates these practices so much—not because he's threatened, but because he sees those he loves getting sucked into a lie that slows their ability to become all he's dreamed they would be. And, like any good parent, when someone hurts the child he loves, he gets angry:

> Let no one be found among you who sacrifices his son or daughter in the fire, who practices divination or sorcery, interprets omens, *engages in witchcraft, or casts spells*, or who is a medium or spiritist or who consults the dead.

Anyone who does these things is detestable to the LORD ....

Deuteronomy 18:10–12 (emphasis mine)

The proponents of Wicca and witchcraft say their religion has been misunderstood and wrongly maligned. They tell us Wicca is the world's oldest religion and it dates back to a golden age when human beings were wiser, nobler, and closer to God.

Nice words, but not exactly true.

Bits and pieces of Wicca have floated around for hundreds of years, but it wasn't until the mid–twentieth century that people snatched them up and combined them into one popular package. In the 1990s, Wicca gained popularity as millions of teens were introduced to "good" witches through movies, books, and TV shows. These stories portrayed witches as kind, smart, helpful, and most of all, powerful. Much of Wicca's popularity was fueled by our culture's concern for women's rights and for the environment.

Am I suggesting there's something wrong with equal rights for women or a healthy environment?

Of course not. But as we've seen, our enemy often takes important truths and gives them just a little twist to make them false.

In Wicca, support of women's rights becomes worship of "the Goddess."

Likewise, *respect for* nature becomes *worship of* nature (although, technically, it's the worship of gods that infuse themselves in nature).

Margot Adler, whose book *Drawing Down the Moon* is considered by many to be the best introduction to contemporary witchcraft, says the basic tenets of her religion include a belief in the divinity of all (sound familiar?), belief in *many* gods and goddesses (familiar message number two), and relative morals. She writes:

> Thou art Goddess. Thou art God. Divinity is immanent in all nature. It is as much within you as without.
>
> In our culture, which has so long denied and denigrated the feminine as negative, evil, or at best, small and unimportant, women (and men, too) will never understand their own creative strength and divine nature until they embrace the creative feminine, the source of inspiration, the Goddess within.[1]

Wicca also centers around the worship of "Mother Earth" and a belief that the divine is present in every atom of nature. But the apostle Paul writes that God's anger is directed toward those who have "exchanged the truth of God for a lie, and worshiped and served created things rather than the Creator" (Romans 1:25).

So not only does Wicca rip off and shortchange the lives of young women … 'it also rips off God by worshiping what he created instead of worshiping him.

Some Specifics

First of all, it's important to know that Wicca is not satanism or the use of black magic. There's absolutely no worship of Satan or the endorsement of using one's "powers" for evil. Instead young Wiccans are encouraged to use their powers for themselves or for good.

So far, so good, right? Let's continue …

There are few absolutes in the practice of Wicca. Much of it is custom-made by the individual or the coven (four to twenty-six people, with the ideal number being thirteen). They often meet twice a month, on new moons and full moons, with ceremonies calling on the gods, worshiping them, and casting spells. There may be a ceremonial knife, but it's only used symbolically. Other items may include a chalice, cauldron, candles, wine, and a holy circle or pentagram drawn around them. Some practice "skycladding" (performing the rituals in the nude). At home most individuals have a handwritten "Book of Shadows" that is part diary, part use of magical spells and charms.

All these can vary from group to group, and again, nothing sounds too harmful. But now let's look at the fine print …

There are a few elements that all who practice Wicca are encouraged to embrace:

1. WORSHIP OF GODS AND GODDESSES. Wiccans worship gods and goddesses, many of whom are borrowed from the ancient Greeks or Romans, like Diana or Apollo or Mercury; others are Egyptian gods; still others are taken from various cultures. Generally speaking, there are at least two, one male and one female. Often, there are more.

Of course Jesus Christ and the Bible have a slightly different take on this practice. I can think of dozens upon dozens of verses, but the most obvious is the very first of the Ten Commandments: "You shall have no other gods before me" (Exodus 20:3).

2. THE WICCAN REDE. The statement comes in various forms, but it basically reads, "If you don't harm others, do whatever you want." Taken to its extreme, this can mean you can do *anything* you want—enjoy any sin, any perversion. There is no right or wrong. As long as you don't hurt anybody else, anything goes.

Sounds fun … except none of us are smart enough to fully know what's dangerous and what's not. As little children, my kids may resent me for not letting them bike on the freeway at rush hour … until they learn the concept of semi trucks and something called "death." The same is true of the way God watches out for us. His rules are to protect us, not frustrate us. We may not always like it when he tells us we can't do something, but when he labels something as sin, it's because he loves us and knows it will eventually hurt us. There's a lot more love in saying, "Thou shalt not jump off a cliff," than saying, "Sure, take the leap." Or, as the Bible so clearly warns, "For the wages of sin is death …" (Romans 6:23).

3. THE LAW OF RETURN OR THE THREEFOLD LAW. Various versions of this basically say, "Pay attention to the Law of Three. Three times your acts return to thee. This lesson, be sure to learn, thou only gets what thee dost earn."

In short, whatever we do, good or evil, it will return to us three times as much. This is a sweet idea when it comes to us doing good.

But thank God I don't have to carry that belief around when I slip up and do bad things. I'm so glad that Jesus Christ has forgiven me for *all* my mistakes so I don't have to suffer for them, let alone three times as much! That was the whole purpose of Jesus dying on the cross—to suffer for my mess-ups so I wouldn't have to. If I put my trust in him and let him be my Lord (another word could be Boss), he'll erase and remove all of my mistakes ... forever. "As far as the east is from the west, so far has he removed our transgressions from us" (Psalm 103:12). Now that's good news!

4. SPELL CASTING. This is practiced in various ways to various degrees. But, as I've said before, this is the big emotional rip-off ... encouraging young people to think they can take a shortcut to fix their problems. By relying on spells and incantations, instead of solving problems through social interaction or good old-fashioned hard work, they often fall behind others in learning the important skills needed to survive whatever life will throw at them in the future.

Then, of course, there's the supernatural aspect. You know the old saying—"if you play with fire, you can get burned"? Sometimes when people play with this type of darkness (even though it has disguised itself as a good thing), it can backfire with negative results—everything from nightmares to ungrounded fears to emotional and sometimes even physical side effects. Let me stress that this doesn't happen often, but it only stands to reason that the more a person tries to tap into powers opposed to God, the greater her odds are of actually connecting to those powers … and reaping the results.

5. A LACK OF NEED FOR JESUS CHRIST. Since they don't believe the material world is evil and since everyone pays for their sins (three times!), there's no need for someone else to forgive them.

This is the most dangerous aspect of all. It's one thing to be worshiping gods in the woods or casting spells or believing that anything goes, but when it comes to denying Jesus Christ and all that he offers us on the cross, well, then we're talking serious eternal-life stuff. I know we've heard these verses hundreds of times, but read them slowly and think about what they really mean: "For God so loved the world that he gave his one and only Son, that whoever believes in him shall not perish but have eternal life. For God did not send his Son into the world to condemn the world, but to save the world through him" (John 3:16–17).

To turn down this incredible gift of love and stand before God having to pay for every sin I've ever committed … honestly, I can't think of anything worse.

In Conclusion…

Wicca is a relatively new religion made up of odds and ends from various beliefs and superstitions. Though this religion may have reached its height a decade ago, it's still enjoying a strong following. Professor Denise Cush, Head of Religious Studies at Bath Spa University in the UK, has interviewed many young witches as part of her studies on paganism. She identifies what is perhaps the strongest pull to witchcraft for many young women:

"One of the main things I found was that it was about identity. Calling myself a witch or a pagan is saying I'm somebody special … and it seemed to give all of the practitioners a great deal of self-esteem, you know—this is me

"The traditional image of a witch is a powerful woman, so for many of the young women it was an image that they could identify that gave them a feeling of confidence and empowerment. Which they contrasted with some more traditional religions where women haven't necessarily had positions of power."[2] And the empowerment aspect of Wicca has carried over into the fascination with more traditional witchcraft today.

All this to say ... on the surface witchcraft and Wicca look like cool ways to gain power, get in touch with nature, find belonging and enjoy whatever pleasures we want. But a deeper look reveals that it:

- Blatantly disobeys God.
- Emotionally rips off those who are looking for power.
- Promises a freedom that can actually endanger.
- Allows its followers to suffer for their sins.

Once again, the bait looks great—until we bite into it and feel the hook.

If you know someone who's looking into or practicing sorcery or witchcraft, love them. Listen to their needs. Be willing to share how a close friendship with the Creator of the universe can meet those needs and fill their emptiness more than they can ever imagine. Or, as Jesus himself said, "The thief comes only to steal and kill and destroy; I have come that they may have life, and have it to the full" (John 10:10).

---

1. Margot Adler, *Drawing Down the Moon (*Boston: Beacon Press, 1986) ix.
2. Research shows young witch increase" Jo Dwyer. 2008. http://news.bbc.co.uk/local/bristol/hi/people_and_places/religion_and_ethics/newsid_7760000/7760383.stm

11

Vampires and Fantasy Games

No book on the occult would be complete without a look at vampires.

You might be thinking, *Wait a minute. Vampires aren't real. They're pure fantasy—aren't they?*

Well, yes ... and no.

In 2005, Stephenie Meyer wrote a book called *Twilight.* This book, which told the story of a vampire named Edward in love with an ordinary high school student named Bella, captivated readers and quickly became a bestseller. Meyers, a stay-at-home mom and Mormon, went on to write three more books to complete the series. And by October 2010, the Twilight Saga series had sold more than 116 million copies worldwide.

Twilight changed the way people thought about vampires. In the past, vampires had mostly been portrayed as sinister creatures intent on killing to satisfy their blood cravings, but Edward, a vampire who lives on the blood of animals, was presented as a hero … not to mention a swoon-worthy boyfriend. On her website, Meyers recounts the experience that led her to write *Twilight*:

> "I woke up from a very vivid dream. In my dream, two people were having an intense conversation in a meadow in the woods. One of these people was just your average girl. The other person was fantastically beautiful, sparkly, and a vampire. They were discussing the difficulties inherent in the facts that A) they were falling in love with each other while B) the vampire was particularly attracted to the scent of her blood, and was having a difficult time restraining himself from killing her immediately."[1]

Meyers had that dream in 2002. Seven years later, she reported having another encounter with Edward:

> "I had this dream that Edward actually showed up and told me that I got it all wrong and like he exists and everything but he couldn't live off animals … and I kind of got the sense he was going to kill me. It was really terrifying and bizarrely different from every other time I've thought about his character."[2]

Although *Twilight* may be nothing more than a compelling story, the obsession with vampires that it has created, along with their not-so-subtle use of occult powers, should give us pause. In her article, "The Darkness of Twilight," Sue Bohlin makes some interesting observations:

> "The *Twilight* vampires all have various kinds of powers that don't come from God. They are supernaturally fast, supernaturally strong, able to read others' minds and control others' feelings. Some can tell the future, others can see things at great distances. These aspects of the occult are an important part of what makes *Twilight* so successful.
>
> "One of the reasons *Twilight* is so dangerous is that readers can

long for these kinds of supernatural but ungodly powers; if not in real life, then in their imagination. And this is a doorway to the demonic, which is all about gaining power from a source other than God. *Twilight* glorifies the occult, the very thing God calls detestable (Deut. 18:9)."[3]

Vampire Wannabes

It's sometimes easy to blur the line between fantasy and reality. True vampires may not exist, but there are people who *think* they're vampires. And they may create just as many problems and be just as lost as if they really were "children of the night."

In 1998, the *Los Angeles Times* carried this story from the Associated Press:

> DALLAS—Four teenagers claiming to be vampires went on a drug-crazed rampage, vandalizing dozens of cars and homes, spray-painting racial slurs and burning a church, police said.
>
> Fascinated by the occult, the teens smoked methamphetamine-laced marijuana before going on a spree through the quiet middle-class neighborhood and causing $300,000 in damage Thursday, officers said.
>
> The fire destroyed the office and fellowship hall at Bethany Lutheran Church. Its outside walls were scrawled with satanic graffiti in pink and white paint.

The article goes on:

> The Dallas Morning News reported that one teen told detectives that he and the others were vampires. The teenagers had marks on their arms from sucking one another's blood, the newspaper reported.[4]

Just a week earlier another story in the *Times* told an even more disturbing story. A seventeen-year-old boy was sentenced to die in the electric chair in Florida after he was convicted of killing a middle-aged couple with a crowbar. Rodrick Justin Ferrell admitted to the murders and said he killed the couple because he is a vampire.

In imposing the death sentence, Lake County Circuit Judge Jerry T. Lockett said the case proves there is "genuine evil in the world." Ferrell was allegedly the leader of a group of teenagers who engaged in orgies and drank blood because they considered themselves to be vampires. Allegedly, the dead couple's daughter wanted to run away with the group and had asked them to help her steal her parents' car. She was not charged in the murders.[5]

These are extreme examples. Cases of "wannabe vampires" who actually suck human blood or kill people are rare. The truth is these shouldn't be our biggest concern. Instead, we should consider what fuels our fascination, and at times obsession, with vampires.

A Bigger Concern

Katherine Ramsland, a forensic psychologist and author of *The Science of Vampires*, explained what she sees as the allure of vampires to ABC News:

"The vampire image is sexy because it's a trespass. It's not just kissing, it's biting ... the vampire has the ability to make you want it, even though you're frightened of it."[6]

As with other areas of the occult, vampirism—even as fantasy—incorporates a strong component of sexual deviance. Trespass is the idea of taking something by force or against the other person's will, which is the same concept behind abuse and rape. Though Meyer's vampire may be able to control himself, his very being—following Bella, watching her sleep, brooding over her—is driven by the urge to trespass and destroy.

Sound familiar?

And, equally as alarming, the stories are created in such a way that Bella actually hungers and yearns to be trespassed upon and destroyed.

Clearly, immersion in vampire culture can be dangerous. While actual vampires may not exist, fantasy vampires do—in the minds of those whose obsession with the dark side of the supernatural may be attempting to control their thoughts and lives.

Good Days for Vampires

J. Gordon Melton, an authority on vampires who wrote *The Vampire Book*, told me that interest in vampires reached its lowest point in 1983. But since then, there has been a tremendous resurgence of interest in "the living dead." The bestselling books written by Anne Rice had a strong impact on this increased interest. Her vampire-oriented novels are mysterious, brooding, romantic, and very sensuous. They have paved the way for a number of books for teenagers that glorify vampires, including *Twilight*, the House of Night series, and The Vampire Diaries. The authors of these books portray vampires in ways that are very appealing to teenagers—especially to those who feel isolated from their peers and are drawn to the romanticism of these stories.

But what if there really was Somebody like that. Not the counterfeit somebody as portrayed in these novels. But Somebody interested in everything about us – our every thought, our every fear, our every desire?

In her book *Escaping the Vampire*, Kimberly Powers explains why young women in particular may be so drawn to the Twilight Saga's love story:

"What if our hearts were created to long for this love because it is actually out there longing for us? What if our souls were shaped for Someone? Someone amazing, who is incredibly attentive to our every need and will treat us better than we could ever imagine. Someone always present in our lives who experiences life with us.

"You can see the charm of Edward and all he is for Bella. Imagine having that type of relationship connection in your life. For some, this may be a radical thought to wrap your mind around—but imagine that this iconic, hunky, bad-boy hero Edward could be outdone so easily by an eternally loving, fiercely protective Savior."[7]

A Savior, who instead of trespassing on you, took your trespasses upon himself (2 Corinthians 5:19).

Vampires Next Door?

In addition to the books, films and TV shows, vampire-oriented clubs have sprung up in America's largest cities, many of them catering to young male homosexuals. Also, teenage girls dress in costume and hold parties or events where they make believe they're vampires. You may see many of these youths wearing capes and fake fangs. Some have even filed their teeth for a more realistic look.

So what?

It's just fantasy, isn't it? What's wrong with that?

At first glance it doesn't appear to be a problem ...

The problem comes when a select few of the kids caught up in these "vampire games" become absorbed by the fantasy and have difficulty telling where reality ends and fantasy begins.

Even my professional actor friends tell me that sometimes

they get so deep into a role that they begin to think and act like the character they're playing. If this is possible for seasoned and experienced actors, imagine how such role-playing can affect impressionable teenagers still searching for their own identities.

Joan Hake Robie, who has spent years researching the dangers of fantasy games and role-playing activities, says that "shared fantasies" are especially dangerous: "Persons who feel inadequate, bored, or alienated from society can be brought into a position where ... alternative realities are much more exciting and fulfilling than real life."[8] She says the result of this can be "withdrawal from society, paranoia, and suppressed or expressed hostility."

Do you remember how David Berkowitz, the Son of Sam from chapter four, got sucked into satanism? He was a loner, an outcast who just didn't fit in ... until his fellow satanists welcomed him into their circle.

Variations of this story are repeated over and over again in every area of occult experience and practice.

This is especially true in vampirism. A very high percentage of those who become involved in vampire fantasies are abused children and teenagers who identify strongly with victims of fantasy vampire attacks—lonely, alienated young people who are simply looking for a caring friend or who want to have some power in their lives. Sadly, as a result, many of them become involved in the occult.

How It All Began

Some experts believe the vampire story was first created in the Middle Ages as a means to enforce proper burial procedures and stop the spread of deadly diseases. According to this belief, if bodies weren't buried deep enough, they could come out of their graves and walk the streets as "the undead," looking for victims.

In short, vampire legends may have started as the result of an over-the-top local health-department campaign. But there were other less civic-minded individuals whose actions perpetuated the myth.

For example, the Countess Erzsebet Bathory of Hungary is said to have drunk and bathed in the blood of more than six hundred young girls in the belief that the practice would keep her eternally young and healthy.[9]

Thanks to the novel by Bram Stoker, the most famous of all vampires is Dracula. Stoker based his character on the life of a Romanian prince named Vlad Dracul, a despicably cruel man otherwise known as Vlad the Impaler, who lived in the rural region of Transylvania, Romania the 1400s. Dracul was a man of amazing cruelty and, driven by political ambition, murdered thousands of people—including many women and children—by impaling them on long stakes. Their bodies were then displayed on roads around his castle as a warning to others who dared to challenge Dracul's authority. Research also indicates that he was a student of the occult.

Manuela Dunn Mascetti, in her book *Vampire: The Complete Guide to the World of the Undead*, writes:

> Dracula decapitated, cut off noses, ears, sexual organs, limbs; he nailed hats to heads; he blinded, strangled, hanged, burned, boiled, skinned, roasted, hacked and buried alive. It is suspected that he practiced cannibalism himself, eating the limbs of those he killed, and drinking their blood; it has been proven that he forced others to eat human flesh.[10]

Dracul reportedly killed somewhere between forty thousand to one hundred thousand people during his lifetime. No wonder he came to be regarded as a supernatural monster. Even after his death peasants in the surrounding countryside were afraid of him. What if Dracul wasn't really dead, but merely looking for a new way to spy on and punish those who spoke against him? Or, worse yet, what if his spirit was still roaming the Transylvanian countryside, looking for more victims to satisfy his bloodlust?

Knowingly or unknowingly, this is the type of character young people pay their respects to when they wear fake fangs and visit vampire clubs.

What About Other Fantasies?

We've seen that vampire fantasies can be dangerous. What about other types of fantasies? Can they be harmful too? After all, we all have daydreams. Is it really so wrong to leave the real world behind for a while?

Psychologists tell us that it all depends on what you spend your time fantasizing about—and on how real your fantasies become. They also say that when a person spends too much time in a fantasy world, it becomes harder to distinguish the real world from the make-believe one.

Some experts believe that it's unhealthy if we spend too much time playing role-playing games—including the type you can buy at stores or play online—particularly if those games include strong violence or incorporate elements of the occult.

When I began to hear people complain about these games, my first reaction was, "Give me a break. It's just a game." But when I started looking at some of the elements in those games and reading people's concerns, I realized they might have a point.

We've already seen how Satan will use any means available to lure people into his realm. And, according to Dr. Gary North, author of *None Dare Call it Witchcraft*, these games let people lose their sense of reality very easily:

> After years of study of the history of occultism, after having researched [for] a book on the subject, and after having consulted with scholars in the field of historical research, I can say with confidence: these games are the most effective, most magnificently packaged, most profitably marketed, most thoroughly researched introduction to the occult in man's recorded history.[11]

Does that mean I think every person who plays fantasy games is involved with the occult? Of course not. But imagine immersing yourself for hours upon hours in a game where you are:

- violently murdering people
- casting magic spells
- using dark, supernatural powers
- worshiping demonic entities
- pretending you're supernaturally evil

It doesn't matter how strong we are—how could a steady diet of thinking, playing, and acting like that *not* affect us?

What Does the Bible Say?

Jesus had a lot to say about the importance of our thinking right. In fact, in Matthew 5, he says:

> "You have heard that it was said to the people long ago, 'You shall not murder, and anyone who murders will be subject to judgment.' But I tell you that anyone who is angry with his brother or sister will be subject to judgment.... You have heard that it was said, 'You shall not commit adultery.' But I tell you that anyone who looks at a woman lustfully has already committed adultery with her in his heart."
>
> Matthew 5:21–28

You see, what we think *is* important.

And we have to be careful about any practice that causes us to think and dwell on things that are wrong or evil. And while I'm quoting the Bible, check these two verses out:

> Take captive every thought to make it obedient to Christ.
>
> 2 Corinthians 10:5

> Do not conform to the pattern of this world, but be transformed by the renewing of your mind.
>
> Romans 12:2

These are the reasons the fascination with vampires and some fantasy games is such a concern. If the Bible's teaching is accurate, then *what we think really does shape* what we do and who we become.

1. "The Story Behind Twilight," The Official Website of Stephenie Meyer, http://www.stepheniemeyer.com/twilight.html

2. "Stephenie Meyer Reveals New Details of Dream About Edward Cullen," March 29, 2009, http://www.twilightgear.net/Twilight-news-and-gossip/stephenie-meyer-reveals-details-of-new-dream-about-edward-cullen/2493

3. "The Darkness of Twilight" by Sue Bohlin, 2010, http://www.probe.org/site/c.fdKEIMNsEoG/b.6099193/k.76B1/The_Darkness_of_Twilight.htm

4. Associated Press, "'Vampires' Burn Church, Police Say," *Los Angeles Times*, March 7, 1998.

5. Donald P. Baker, "Judge Cites Genuine Evil, Gives Death Sentence to Youth, 17," *Los Angeles Times*, February 28, 1998.

6. "Real-Life Vampires: Who Are They?" by Ki Mae Heussner, *ABC News* October 31, 2008: http://abcnews.go.com/Technology/story?id=6154446&page=1

7. *Escaping the Vampire* by Kimberly Powers, David C. Cook, 2009, pg. 27

8. Joan Hake Robie, *The Truth About Dungeons & Dragons* (Lancaster, PA: Starburst Publishers, 1991) 69.

9. Manuela Dunn Mascetti, *Vampire: The Complete Guide to the World of the Undead* (New York: Penguin Books, 1992) 97.

10. Mascetti, 150.

11. Robie, 24.

12

More Doors to be Wary of Opening

There are lots of other occult beliefs out there. And, like we've said before, the same pattern emerges over and over again … particularly:

1. We don't need Jesus to take the punishment for our mistakes.
2. We can become God-like on our own.
3. Jesus Christ was a good teacher, but definitely not God the Son.

Most of these come under the heading of New Age. The ones we'll take a quick look at are:

- Channeling
- Astrology
- Astral projection
- Yoga

- Meditation
- Crystal power
- Extrasensory perception
- Universalism

Channeling

Channeling is nothing new. It's the same thing spirit mediums have been doing for centuries—giving control of their bodies and minds to unseen entities who speak through them. As we've seen these entities sometimes claim to be spirits of the dead, angels, or aliens from advanced civilizations in outer space.

The entities that speak through New Age channelers are only different in that they claim they are ancient spirits who have evolved over thousands of years and who have come back to share their wisdom.

We just mentioned Satan's three favorite lies. Let's take a look at a couple of recent history's most popular channeled entities and see how their teachings match up. By the way, if you haven't read chapter three, now might be a good time to give it a look.

Seth

Seth began speaking through a woman named Jane Roberts in the 1960s. From that time until her death in 1984, Roberts produced a number of books bearing Seth's name that have sold millions of copies.

Roberts first began to channel "Seth" when she and her husband were writing a book on extrasensory perception. They were using a Ouija board to do research for their book when they began to receive messages from someone who identified himself as Frank Withers. Soon Withers changed his mind about his identity, explaining, "I prefer not to be called Frank Withers. That personality was rather colorless. You may call me whatever you choose. I call myself Seth. It fits the me of me, the personality more clearly approximating the whole self I am, or am trying to be."[1]

Seth described himself as "an energy personality essence no longer focused in physical reality."[2]

Most of the books "Seth" wrote were dictated through Roberts' voice while she was in a trance. Writing as Seth she says, "You are given the gift of the gods; you create your reality according to your beliefs; yours is the creative energy that makes your world; there are no limitations to the self except those you believe in."[3]

Is it my imagination, or does this sound a lot like, "You have within you the power to become like God"?

Ramtha

Seth's books continue to sell today, but ... around 1985 Ramtha showed up ... and he's stuck around. Ramtha claims to be a thirty-five-thousand-year-old spirit and calls himself "the enlightened one." He's channeled by a woman named JZ Knight, who claims a psychic told her that the "Enlightened One" would appear to her in the future.[4] Ramtha seems to love the spotlight. He makes numerous public appearances, where he gives convoluted advice to wide-eyed believers who have paid up to one thousand dollars apiece for the privilege of hearing his wisdom.

Ramtha claims to have lived on Lemuria, an ancient but highly advanced civilization that sank into the Pacific Ocean eons ago. There's no evidence to prove that Lemuria ever existed, but Ramtha's devotees completely believe it.

In his book *Channeling*, author Jon Klimo describes Ramtha's appearances:

> Knight goes into a deep or cataleptic trance, calming her body so that "Ramtha," a powerful male presence, can enter. "Ramtha"

speaks in a somewhat archaic, stylized manner, claiming to have been incarnated 35,000 years ago as a spiritual and political leader known as "The Ram" who came from fabled Lemuria into what is now India …

"Ramtha's" theme is that we are like gods; part of God, yet unconscious of this identity. Nonetheless, we create our own realities within which to express ourselves, against which to react, from which to learn, and in which to evolve. This is a view that is virtually identical with the "Seth" teachings as well as with many other channeled materials.[5]

Sound familiar? Like so many others, Ramtha insists we must learn to "worship" ourselves:

The reason that I am here is to tell you how important that you are. Because the only way that one enters into the Kingdom of Heaven, 'tis not through the worship of another but the worship of the All. And the only way you can ever comprehend the All is from your point of view. And your point of view is called God and that is where you find Him. How do you think, my beloved people, that you ever become? By following someone else, by worshiping something you never saw and never understood? You become by worshiping you.[6]

And, of course, Ramtha also seems to claim a special "god-likeness" for himself:

I choose to come back in this fashion in this embodiment as a woman, not to demonstrate that a man and a woman can live together peacefully—they can—but [to demonstrate] that God is both man and woman, equally and evenly. [I choose to come back in this fashion] to not leave you any images that you could bolt around your neck or put up on your wall or carve into stone, because you have always been notorious for worshiping others.[7]

Sounds like a little reverse psychology. "Okay, you got me ... I'm a god ... but don't worship me. And whatever you do, don't worship anyone else ... except, of course, the god that lies within."

As we see, there's nothing at all new about entities such as Ramtha or the messages they bring. Incidentally, Douglas James Mahr, who was once Ramtha's "chosen scribe" and recorded the words of Ramtha quoted above, has since become a Christian and no longer believes in the message or the power of "the enlightened one."

Astrology

Astrology says that our personalities and our lives are governed by the position of the stars and planets. Most people will tell you they don't put much faith in astrology. But nearly every major daily newspaper in America carries an astrology column and a daily horoscope—and they wouldn't waste the space if people didn't read them. A Pew Forum report reveals that 25 percent of Americans and 23 percent of Christians believe in astrology.[8]

Astrology is a form of fortune-telling that subtly denies the power of God. Boil it down to its basic essence, and it teaches that we're dependent on the position of the stars and planets rather than the grace and will of God.

God himself mocks the practice of astrology when he says through the prophet Isaiah:

> Let your astrologers come forward, those stargazers who make predictions month by month, let them save you from what is coming upon you. Surely they are like stubble; the fire will burn them up. They cannot even save themselves from the power of the flame.
>
> Isaiah 47:13–14

Besides denying the power of God, astrology isn't true for

several other reasons. The most important of these is that the entire belief system was constructed on the mistaken idea that the stars rotate around the earth. Also there are huge disagreements among astrologers regarding the nature of the signs of the zodiac, which are essential in mapping out an individual's horoscope. Some astrologers believe there are eight signs of the zodiac, while others insist there are twelve, some fourteen, and still others twenty-four.

Obviously astrology is anything but an exact science.

Some people get hooked on it because it seems to work, at least part of the time. Of course it does. You'd have to be an unbelievably terrible fortune-teller to be wrong all the time. Besides, a lot of events related to astrology may simply be self-fulfilling. Someone gets up in the morning and reads his horoscope. It tells him he's going to have a rough day. So he goes off to work thinking, *I'll sure be glad when this day is over.* He expects the worst, and he makes it happen. He performs sloppily on the job, he thinks others are out to get him, and at the first sign of any trouble, he throws up his hands and says, "I knew today was going to stink!"

But the main reason to avoid astrology is that God is against it when he says:

> When you look up to the sky and see the sun, the moon and the stars—all the heavenly array—do not be enticed into bowing down to them and worshiping things the LORD your God has apportioned to all the nations under heaven.
>
> Deuteronomy 4:19

Astral Projection

Astral projection, or "soul travel," is the belief that we as human beings can project our souls out of our bodies at will. There are classes where students are supposedly taught how to do this through controlled breathing, meditation, visualization, and other occult-oriented techniques.

In preparing for this book, I watched an instructional video from one of these classes. The instructor laughed as he told his students that soul travel was such a natural occurrence to him that he often forgot to take his body with him. Just the other night, he said, he had decided to get out of bed and go into the kitchen for a snack. It wasn't until he reached for the doorknob and it went right through his hand that he realized he had left his body lying on the bed.

His eager, young students all laughed, obviously anxious for the day when they, too, would become adept at astral projection.

But is it really possible to treat my body like an overcoat, putting it on and taking it off at will?

In California a researcher named Dr. Charles Tart achieved mixed results when he conducted experiments with a woman who was supposedly adept at astral projection. She was asked to "travel" into another area to read a number that had been written on a piece of paper.

She was correct only one out of four attempts.[9]

Not very impressive. Dr. Tart did say, however, on one occasion, the woman seemed able to read a clock that was not visible from where she sat. Now we're talking two out of five. Forty percent. Still not terribly convincing.

Nothing in the Bible specifically forbids astral projection. But if it's possible to judge a philosophy by the company it keeps—in this instance, communication with departed spirits and reincarnation—then soul travel isn't something I'd encourage anyone to try. It's an occult-type experience that, if sought after, can open the door to other, more clearly dangerous practices.

Whether or not soul travel is actually possible, I certainly believe that our enemy can cause an illusion and make it seem to happen. As a result, people who are seeking after this experience may be seeking something that can be dangerous and deceptive.

Some who believe in astral projection point to occurrences in the Bible where God supernaturally moved people great distances in an instant. For example, the eighth chapter of Acts contains the account of Philip's conversion of the Ethiopian eunuch. The Bible says that after the eunuch was baptized, "When they came up out of the water, the Spirit of the Lord suddenly took Philip away, and the eunuch did not see him again, but went on his way rejoicing. Philip, however, appeared at Azotus, and traveled about, preaching the gospel in all the towns until he reached Caesarea" (Acts 8:39–40).

There is *no way* this can be construed as soul travel. Philip was in one place, and then the next moment, he was somewhere far away—body, soul, and spirit. Philip's *entire being* traveled, not just his soul.

I once heard a man who was a medical missionary to Africa tell about a similar experience. He was in his office, catching up on some paperwork, when some villagers came running in, yelling for him to come quick because one of their friends had suddenly fallen ill. The missionary grabbed his bag and ran out of his office, and the next thing he knew, he was running up to the sick man's hut. He had instantaneously covered a distance of nearly three miles.

The villagers who had come to enlist his help later told him that they had seen him come running out of his house, but that he had then immediately vanished. The situation was urgent, so God supplied the means of travel.

But again, it wasn't merely this man's soul that traveled but all of him. And he hadn't sought the experience. God gave it when it was needed.

Yoga

Yoga can be, but isn't always, another component of the New Age package. Some adherents insist that yoga is simply a series of exercises and meditations designed to keep the body and mind healthy. It's just a way to stay fit, they say, and what could be wrong with that? On the surface, nothing. And if a person stays at that level, there's probably little harm. But those who have studied yoga closely say it goes much deeper. Real Yoga is more than a way to stay fit. It's a Hindu form of worship.

The Merriam-Webster's Collegiate Dictionary says that Yoga is "a Hindu theistic philosophy teaching the suppression of all activity of body, mind, and will in order that the self may realize its distinction from them and attain liberation."[10]

Douglas Hunt, in his pro-occult book *Exploring the Occult*, says, "*Yoga* means much the same word as *yoke* in English, and it is a system designed to link the human with the source of his being. In other words, it has almost exactly the same meaning as the word *religion*, which also is supposed to yoke man to his Master."[11]

One wonders which Master.

He laments the fact that Westerners don't always see the religious "benefits" Yoga has to offer and that we're "seldom able to look at anything more than the physical or material aspect of anything."[12]

But refusing to look at the religious aspects of Yoga doesn't make them go away. If someone says to me, "I know Yoga involves worshiping Hindu gods, but I'm not serious about that, so it's okay for me," my response is, "You might be right." Still, if you go deeper and look at the root of the practice, it's impossible to miss the fact that Yoga is directly connected to false gods, and for that reason, it could be potentially dangerous.

For example, one of the most important aspects of Yoga is mind-emptying ...

Meditation

Unlike biblical meditation, where we're encouraged to fill our minds with God and his Word, Eastern meditation encourages us to empty our minds.

And that's a huge difference.

Let me tell you about Mark …

Like many of us, he was running as fast as he could, only to get further and further behind. The stress became so bad that he couldn't sleep more than a few hours at night. He lost his appetite. There was a constant tightness in his chest and a burning sensation in his stomach.

A coworker suggested he try Eastern meditation. His friend told him he had tried it himself, and it had calmed him down, given him a positive outlook, and helped him learn to cope with day-to-day frustrations.

It sounded great. Even though Mark remembered something about this form of meditation involving "mystical" religious practices, it didn't bother him. He was ready to try anything and figured that meditation had to be better than a daily dose of Prozac.

Mark found that meditation was everything his coworker said it would be. Almost immediately he felt renewed and relaxed. He meditated as often as he could … even at work. He would close the door of his office, recite his mantra, and leave his worries behind. Even though Mark was a dedicated Christian, he wondered how he had ever managed to get by before he had discovered meditation.

At his deepest, most peaceful moments, he felt he had made contact with benevolent spirits from beyond this world—beings that were beautiful, loving, and full of joy and peace.

It got to the point where it was easy for Mark to slip into a dreamlike state. It was almost like a trance.

And that's when he had the vision.

On a quiet, still evening, all alone in his living room, Mark had an encounter with something evil—something that had been waiting for him in the depths of his meditation experiences.

I said it was a vision. Mark wasn't so sure. To him the creature was suddenly in the room with him, urging him deeper and deeper into the trance-like state, mocking him and daring him to just try to regain control of his life.

"I was aware," he told me, "that I was falling into the hands of someone who I didn't want to even touch me."

"Was it Satan?" I asked.

"If it wasn't, it came pretty darn close."

"Why did the 'creature' choose that moment to reveal himself?"

"I have no idea. Maybe they figured I was so far gone that they had me, so they had nothing to lose by revealing themselves to me."

"*Themselves?*" I asked.

"The ones who are behind it all," he said. "Satan and his demons."

Crystal Power

This is a fad that comes and goes. Are crystals dangerous? No more than your average rabbit's foot or four-leaf clover. But they can be very big in the New Age world and are supposed to attract positive energy, bringing health and luck.

No surprise.

Crystals have been an important part of the occult for centuries. Every self-respecting fortune-teller has traditionally had a crystal ball to "reveal secrets" about the future.

I suppose it's easy to see why crystals have such attraction. They're beautiful. They're geometrically perfect. They can break white light into a dazzling display of colors. They can convert radio-frequency energy into audio-frequency energy. And they make beautiful drinking glasses.

But they're not magical.

I've been in South American and African countries where the poor have all kinds of charms and good luck pieces they put their hope and trust in. We can call them superstitious. We can call them primitive. But couldn't these items just as easily be crystals?

Now that still doesn't say there's anything wrong with the New Age interest in crystals, does it?

No.

The problem is when someone looks to a crystal to keep him safe, healthy, and prosperous. He has given that crystal the place in his life that God deserves. It's become a type of idol, and we all have a pretty good idea of how God feels about idols.

ESP and Psychic Research

Like the crystals we've been talking about, extrasensory perception and psychic research can be judged by the company they keep. They're usually lumped together with things like fortune-telling and spirit communication. As a result interest in extrasensory perception may invariably lead to an interest in other, more deeply occult matters.

When I was researching my novel *Threshold*, I was amazed at the amount of time and money scientists were devoting to the study of ESP. The CIA alone had spent more than twenty million dollars and over twenty years of research. In many instances the results are quite impressive, proving by science what we already know by faith—the existence of a supernatural world.

That's the good news. The bad news is that more often than not, these well-meaning men and women are entering the world of the occult without even knowing it.

I'll never forget visiting one of the top psychic research labs in the world as it carried out an extensive ESP experiment. There, at the center of their experiment, sat a Ouija board. (Check out chapter six if you haven't already).

ESP, psychic research, and other dabblings in the occult—regardless of our intentions or intellect—are risky ventures. And my advice to these folks is the same as to anyone else: Don't get involved.

If we play with the devil's fire, we'll eventually get burned.

Universalism

There are lots of other beliefs and practices that fall under the heading of New Age. But the final one I want to discuss is *universalism*, the belief that all religions ultimately lead to God and that everyone will eventually be saved. People who subscribe to this belief consider traditional Christianity to be narrow-minded and divisive. I understand their position. But if it comes down to me believing in what the latest fad teachings and trends say or in what Jesus Christ himself says, I'm putting my trust in the man who raised himself (and three others) from the dead and who most people claim to be one of the greatest teachers of all time.

And, according to him, there's *only one way* to heaven:

> I am the way and the truth and the life. No one comes to the Father except through me.
>
> John 14:6

> For God so loved the world that he gave his one and only Son, that whoever believes in him shall not perish but have eternal life . . . Whoever believes in him is not condemned, but whoever does not believe stands condemned already because they have not

believed in the name of God's one and only Son.

John 3:16, 18

I am the resurrection and the life. The one who believes in me will live, even though they dies; and whoever lives by believing in me will never die.

John 11:25–26

You can't get much clearer than that.

So what have we learned about the "New Age"? Simply that there's nothing new about it.

At best it's a marketing campaign, an attempt to take some of the oldest tricks in the book and dress them up in shiny new packages. At worst it comes from our enemy, the father of lies, who's always looking for a new angle to steal, kill, and destroy.

---

1. Klimo, 30.
2. Klimo, 30.
3. Klimo, 29.
4. Knight, J.Z., (1987). *A State of Mind: My Story.* New York: Warner books.
5. Klimo, 43.
6. Ramtha, with Douglas James Mahr, *Voyage to the New World* (New York: Ballantine Books, 1985) 275.
7. Ramtha/Mahr, 274–275.
8. "Many Americans Mix Multiple Faiths," December 9, 2009, http://pewforum.org/Other-Beliefs-and-Practices/Many-Americans-Mix-Multiple-Faiths.aspx
9. Randles and Hough, 213–214.
10. "Yoga," Merriam-Webster's Collegiate Dictionary Online, 11th edition, accessed February 15, 2012. http://www.merriam-webster.com/dictionary/yoga
11. Douglas Hunt, *Exploring the Occult* (New York: Ballantine Books, 1964) 138.
12. Hunt, 138.

13

Wrapping Up

So we're at the end of a very brief journey through the dark side of the supernatural.

I haven't tried to cover every topic, and I know that much of what we've done here has only been skimming the surface. But everywhere we've looked, we've seen the lies, broken promises, and dangers waiting in the occult.

Still, thousands of people are drawn into it every day.

Why?

Most are looking for answers to the questions:

- Why are we here?
- Is there more to life than what we see on the surface?
- Does life go on beyond the grave?
- How do I fill this supernatural hunger?

The good news is, there are answers … but not through the

counterfeits that are, at best, money-draining deceptions full of double-talk—and at worst, doors leading to destruction.

Remember, according to Jesus Christ, there is someone out there who wants to destroy us:

> "The thief comes only to steal and kill and destroy …"
>
> John 10:10

And he'll do *anything* in his power to seduce us into his territory so he can pounce on us and hurt us.

Thankfully, there's another place we can go, and it's to the one who promises:

> " … I have come that they may have life, and have it to the full."
>
> John 10:10

This is the *only place* God gives us permission for a supernatural encounter … in a personal relationship with his Son, Jesus Christ.

Granted, you don't often get the superficial experiences or the appealing special effects, but that friendship with God and the Son is deeper and more powerful than all those momentary "pleasures" put together. There's a custom-made hole in our souls … a hole that can only be filled by a relationship with God himself.

We're all hungry for something supernatural, and God offers us a huge banquet of the best supernatural food in the universe, while Satan offers us cheap food that's been poisoned to kill us.

If we commit our lives to God, we have nothing to fear. His love is greater than all the forces of darkness put together. If we belong to him, we not only have his love, but also his promise that:

> Neither death nor life, neither angels nor demons, neither the present nor the future, nor any powers, neither height nor depth, nor anything else in all creation, will be able to separate us from the love of God that is in Christ Jesus our Lord.
>
> Romans 8:38–39

Impressive promises that have been proven true to millions of people for twenty centuries.

If you haven't tasted the real food, if you haven't experienced such a friendship and are interested, it's pretty simple …

Step One …

Remember, God is so holy and perfect that none of us are good enough to approach him. That's why he sent his Son down from heaven … to take the punishment for our imperfections so we can be with him. That's what the cross was all about … God paying the bill for all our failures.

Only *after* that payment is made are we clean enough to approach God and start that supernatural relationship with him.

So, first you have to admit your failures and ask Jesus Christ to pay for them.

Step Two …

Next ask God to be your boss (that's what the word *Lord* means).

You have to let him start calling the shots in your life. It's kind of like sliding over in the car and letting him take the steering wheel. It's a wondrous ride, and he'll take you places you never dreamed … but you have to let go.

Will you make mistakes and grab the wheel back from him? You bet. We all do.

But each time, admit what you've done, ask for his forgiveness, and give it back.

Remember, he's on your side. He wants the best for you. And he'll lovingly work with you no matter how bad or how often you make mistakes ... *if* you're serious about admitting them and giving the wheel back to him.

And what does he get out of the deal? Just the satisfaction that you're on your way to becoming all he dreamed you would be when he created you, that you're becoming ...

"mature and complete, *not lacking anything.*"

James 1:4, emphasis mine

What a tremendous gift!

God not only picks up the tab for our failures, but he'll stay with us, be our friend, and make us "mature and complete, not lacking anything." That's a far cry from the thief who wants to "steal and kill and destroy."

But ...

The Choice Is Ours

He's not going to come barging into our lives, demanding we let Jesus forgive us of our failures or let him be the boss.

We have to ask. We have to let him.

If you haven't made that commitment, give it some thought. Pray about it. Talk to people you trust who have made it. And finally, check out what Jesus has to say about it. (The Gospel of John is a good place to start.)

Asking Christ to forgive your sins and take control of your life is a serious commitment and not to be taken lightly. But when you make that commitment, I promise you this: Your life will be fuller than you could ever imagine, because it will no longer just be you living your life. God will be right there with you, every step of the way, as a loving Friend who will never leave you.

God Thrives on Truth

There's always a danger when condensing so much research into a single book. At times the information may seem simplistic, or worse, judgmental and unloving. Being unloving isn't my intent. But it takes more love to warn someone that their building is on fire than to say nothing and just let them sit there as the flames trap and destroy them.

If I've stepped on a toe or if you disagree with any of my conclusions, *please*, do the research yourself. And check the Scriptures. But don't just buy the latest fad or fall for something because it looks all bright and sparkly. (That's how bug zappers work.)

Dig deep until you get to the bedrock of truth ... because God thrives on truth. There will always be liars and con artists out there to deceive you, but if you keep seeking truth, I promise you, you'll eventually find it.

More importantly, you'll eventually find him.

If you feel you're already too deep into some of the practices we've discussed and can't get free on your own, talk to someone who knows the "Great Liberator" ... or begin talking to him yourself, because helping to set people free is one of Jesus' specialties. Or as he says, he's come to "proclaim freedom for the prisoners ... to set the oppressed free ..." (Luke 4:18). Or, to those who seek and believe in him: "You will know the truth, and the truth will set you free" (John 8:32).

Again ... pray, read, and seek mature men and women of God for help. Churches are a great place to find folks willing to lend a hand. Or a Bible study. Or a friend's youth group. Find them, because they're willing to help. And help *will* come. Not necessarily overnight. Usually, it's a step at a time. But every time you reach out to Christ for help, he'll be there for you. He's paid too great a price on the cross to ignore you or let you slip through his fingers. Just keep reaching out to him as best you know how. He'll do all the rest.

He always has.

He always will.

It comes with his all-consuming love for you.